Listen To The Wild

Gail Rudd Entrekin
Editor

1996
California Poets in the Schools

© 1996 California Poets in the Schools
All rights reserved
Printed in the United States of America
Cover design by Lee Ann Brook
Cover illustration 'Living Spirits' by Sondra Spann, 6th grade:
"*Living Spirits* shows wild spirit women dancing in the spirit world. They've died and most of them are swirling in the wind. One is kneeling down and praying. Around some of them there are still pools of blood. There are the freed spirits, and the bodies left behind."
         Sondra Spann, Magnolia Middle School

ISBN # 0-939927-13-6

California Poets in the Schools is grateful to the hundreds of individuals, foundations and agencies who offer their support; among them include:

California Arts Council	Tina Demirdjian
Richard F. Dwyer—Eleanor W. Dwyer Fund	Janet Grande
Familia Diaz Restaurant	Surlene Grant
Fireman's Fund Foundation	Holly Hendrickson
The Follett Foundation	Irma Kalman
The Gap Foundation	Tobey Kaplan
The Gerbode Foundation	Susan Kline
The Goodworks Foundation	Betty Kulp
Lafayette Arts & Science Foundation	Allan Lasher
Lakeshore PTA	David and Lynn Crosbia Loux
Lannan Foundation	Ann & Carl Ludwig
Marin Community Foundation	Dorothy Lykes
Mill Valley Community Foundation	Stephen Massicotte
Mountain View PTA	Brian Smith & Alison McLean
National Endowment for the Arts	Stephanie Mendel
Poets & Writers Foundation	John Morton & Laura Donnelly
Robinson Properties ExPress	Charles & Nancy McLaughlin
(In memory of poet Lu Melander)	Jackie Mundell
San Francisco Arts Commission	Amy & David Nelson
Santa Clara Arts Commission	Johnnierenee Nelson
The Society for Excellence in Education	Patricia Nichols
Sonoma County Community Fund	Chris Olander
Sunkist PTA of Oxnard	Dr. Jane Oldden
City of Oakland	Patagonia, Inc.
Bay Paul Foundation	Stephen Rentmeesters
Cultural Council of Santa Cruz	Adrienne Rich
The Vanguard Public Foundation	Ivy & Leigh Robinson
City of Ventura	Susan Roegiers
William James Association	Jean Schulz
Witter Bynner Foundation for Poetry	Don Shanley
The Zellerbach Foundation	Ruth & Dunham Sherer
Anonymous	Susan Herron Sibbet
Duane BigEagle	David Simons
Albert Daniel Brockman	Lani Steele
Elizabeth & Park Chamberlain	Susan Sterling
Daryl & Phyllis Chinn	Judith Stronach
Carla Cogan	Janet Traub
Deborah Costello	Helen Wickes
Robert Cox	Lilla & Andrew Weinberger
Day Studio-Workshop, Inc.	Janice J. Wilson

Table of Contents

INTRODUCTION, Pamela Satterwhite 5
EDITOR'S NOTES, Gail Rudd Entrekin 7
DEDICATION: To Jenny Gealey 11

SECTION ONE: WILD WORLD
The Storm, Elena Garza 17
To Live, Zoe Meharg 18
Lightning, Ms. Huey's kindergarten class 19
Warm Silence, Anna Cameron 20
New Year Poem (for Tan Chi-Wah), John Barbato 21
The Moon I See, Claire Marana 22
Alive, Candace Van Vliet 22
El Granzido Magico / The Magic Quack, Diana Resendiz 23
Sea Song, Claudia Axel 24
Walking with the Wolf, Meagan Banyard 25
The Rain, Zaire Paterson 26
Untitled, Andrea Henry 26
Red Life, Tyson Siddle 27
At Night, Song-I Yang 27
Tender Mountains, Jewinell Barlow 28
Streets, Amber Martin 29
Leaf, Adina Fleming 29
Untitled, Cullen Breuer-Harberts 30
The Rabbit, Christina Girlando 31
Powder Pink, Alexis Mourenza 32
Christmas in a Calvin Klein Jungle, Michael Baker 32
Infinity, Diana Strong 34
In the Sky, Kari Hall 34
In Africa, Brette Gentry 36
City Life of Bombay, Ajay Nayak 37
Van Gogh's "Garden at St. Remy", Jill Fortuna 38
Fields, E.D. 39
The Rain Forest, Tim Lowe 40
Gone, Zack Ziegler 41
Lawn Chairs, Justin 42
Woman, Addie Reyes 43
Staying Warm, Toni Bagley 44
The Lady in Pieces, Mrs. Allen's 1st grade class 45
Cowboy Bill, Evelyn Belasco 46
On My Way Home, Jessy 47
Angel Wings, Yvonne Mason 48
In Autumn, Nereida Gutierrez 49
My Influence, Colleen Bruce 49
Girl at Huck House, Page & Lyon, San Francisco, Teri Marquis 50
With My Apologies, Teri Marquis 52
9 A.M., Mike Carlin 54
Cuando Me Tumbaron / When They Knocked Me Down, Juan Bautista 55
poetry teacher, devorah major 56
Ode, Thomas Centolella 58
Teacher That Shines, Gabriel Catalfo 60

SECTION TWO: WILD MIND

Joy, Thomas Centolella 62
Flash of White Light, Ross Hale 63
Red, Laura Albright-Wirtz 64
The Wink, Chau Ta 66
Flowers and Us, Nixya Velasco 67
Asleep in the House of Art, Ann Marie Samson 68
A Vague Memory, Matthew Ward 69
In My Dream, Sara Heidelberger 70
Wheat, Allison Hedge-Coke 71
Don't Forget to Breathe, Terra Easton 72
Rattlesnake, Albert Linden 73
Soy Jorge / I Am Jorge, Jorge Luis Hernandez 74
Soy Jennifer / I Am Jennifer, Jennifer Vasquez 75
Happiness, Edwina Shin 76
Annelisa's Poem, Annelisa Moe 76
I'm Standing Here, Now, Ryan Steckler 77
Shy, Lauren Reda 78
Shyness, Sharleen Esteves 78
Stutter Stutter, Somkhit Thongban 79
I Am Black, Sprigley Allan 80
My Heart, Simon Christy 80
Vida, Lorena Macias 81
What Can I Do?, LaQuinta Clark 82
Surreal Juxtapositions, Katie Hardin 83
Mama Who, Emily Chan 84
Grandmother, Jeremiah Khaleq 85
Potato Love, Amy Williams 86
Father, Cameron Brooks 87
Finding Life, Felipe Sanchez 88
Roben, Ian Maurer 88
Marc of Courage, Jon Campbell 89
Pact, Karen Benke 90
Alligator Tales, Karen Benke 92
Late 20th Century: Spring, Jerry Martien 93
When I First Saw the Girl, Otto Maldonado 94
Skating Life, Andrew Wike 95
Learning Spanish, Sara Goodrich 96
That Looks Good, Abigail Abiog 97
Simplicity, Jon Campbell 98

ARTICLES
The Pen is Mightier Than the Mouse, Karin Faulkner 100
"Wowbang, Big Fun, Long Day," Jennifer Arin 103
Earth Day: Worshipping Dirt, Terry Ehret 107
Art and Poetry, Glory Foster 111
Writing About Family, Melissa Kwasny 114

BIBLIOGRAPHY 119

Introduction

The wild – what we inherently are – is easy to forget. 'Easy' given our regimented lives, the breakneck pace of them, the so-many rules. Is it any wonder we must turn to the children for maps back to who we really are?

Dear ant.
I am
sorry
that
I ruined
your
home
but
it was
fun...

It makes me drop my eyes to admit but I couldn't tell you how many times I've warned my young son off doing some wonderfully imaginative bit of natural experimentation, exploring the world around him, discovering things in the child's 'messy' way with that exquisite sense of joy, by grimly challenging the utility of his actions ("what are you doing *that* for?") And he would respond with his broad grin, "because it's fun." How terrible!

"Listen to the wild" is a timely admonition. Has there ever been a time in human history when we more needed to listen? a place less amenable to listening? where we're either 'working' sixty hours a week or pacing the streets as cast-offs?

As we rush about the business of survival, barely stopping to glance at our own reflection but never at the world around us, it behooves us to bend our ears and eyes to those among us still able to pay attention: the artists, and the children – the keepers of the sights.

In this collection I think you'll be moved as I was by what our young people notice; how they capture the essence of things ("must find red life;") how they roll perfectly with, and describe, the cycle of life; never losing hope ("a heart breaking, then loving again,") despite the misery around them ("I hear something open the door;") by their triumphant merging with the forces of life around them ("heard my songs bounce off cliffs / and ripple the ocean,") and across generations ("I can taste your heart going through my veins.") Our young people are truly "king[s] of the imagination / who want to write / [they are] eyes." And they are the constant reminders of who we are.

We are...seeking fun, holding sights, singing the songs of childhood in the face of the dullness of adulthood, reaching across a generation gap of joy. As they reach out their hands to us, I hope you'll take them, and turn your back for a time on grim duty and its nagging complaints, answering it simply, "but it was fun."

Editor's Notes

When I was a teen, I occasionally awoke late on a week-end morning to the voice of my father, a Cleveland Transit bus driver, declaiming as he came down the hall:

> Hark! Hark! the lark at heaven's gates sings,
> And Phoebus 'gins arise,
> His steeds to water at those spings
> On chaliced flowers that lies;
> And winking Mary-buds begin
> To ope their golden eyes:
> With everything that pretty is,
> My lady sweet, arise.

Sometimes he stood on the kitchen steps and quoted to his audience of kids and cats the entire "Raven," which he had committed to memory as a high school student. And in my memory there's a clear picture of him brandishing his imaginary sword and crying, "Half a league, half a league, half a league onward, into the valley of death rode the six " An agnostic himself, he often gave me Leigh Hunt's "Abou Ben Adhem" as a bedtime story.

In fourth grade, I recited "The Raven" from memory for my class. Halfway through, my teacher cut me off, no doubt in light of the blanket of boredom which had settled over the classroom. I was incredulous. How could they not understand the drama here? How could she not want to know how it ended? (Something may have been lacking in my delivery.)

All my father's poems and others (not to mention all the lyrics to every popular song from 1960 to 1980) are part of the rich legacy of words stored in my own head all these years later. Memorizing the music of poetry came to me as a normal, natural, and easy thing to do. It was many years before I discovered that this is not so for everyone.

In junior high and high school, all my English teachers but one skipped over the poetry sections or rushed through them telling us not to worry if we didn't get it, "poetry is basically incomprehensible" anyway. And throughout my life thereafter, with the exception of college and grad school years when I was in

English departments, the love of poetry was a solo experience. I wrote and published pretty much in the closet.

On one occasion a friend of mine, a high-powered attorney, remarked on its being the "height of bad taste" to recite a (perfectly non-controversial) poem at a dinner party at her house.

At last, well into my 30s, I met and married my husband, a poet who brought with him a whole community of writers and artists who feel that a poem at table is not a bit extraordinary, but still a treat.

I consider myself lucky to have found a community of friends who believe that poetry, that all art, is a normal and necessary part of a healthy life. This seems so to me, in spite of all the years I spent in the so-called "real world" where art has no part.

William Carlos Williams said, "You cannot get the news from poems/but men die miserably everyday/for lack of what is found there."

What is found there? Well, for one thing, poems fulfill the passionate desire of the unconscious to see the world in metaphorical terms. Doesn't that wiley secret part of our minds constantly find ways to recreate our current life's dilemmas in the metaphorical language of our dreams?

As I attempted to divide the work in this anthology into poems of the inner landscape and poems of the outer one, it became ever more clear to me how inseparable the two worlds are; how our "wild minds" spring directly from the "wild world" we live in; how the metaphors we use to express our feelings leap straight out of the natural world;

how truly we are creatures of the planet.

If you write poetry, you access not only this metaphorical world, but the deep sensory world in which we step out of the chronological order of daily life and into a free space of emotional truth. You drop a line down into the river of feeling that runs below the surface of our lives.

Writing offers us a direct line to our own difficult-to-get-to unconscious. When we write, often we find out what we feel at this single moment in time. Many of us write for this reason alone.

Now I have children of my own, and I want them to have access to this world inside them. I want them to acquire the skills they need to play music and paint and write poems, so that throughout their lives they will have all these options for finding out and expressing to others what is happening in their hearts. In the three Northern California communities in which we have lived, the first two of those arts were being ably presented in the schools, but there was no poetry.

And so I began going into my children's classrooms and declaiming "The Raven" from atop a chair. My father would have been proud. I read Kenneth Koch's classic <u>Wishes, Lies and Dreams</u> and began asking kids to tell me about their dreams, their names, their secret hiding places.

Now they tell me in amazing similes what they themselves are like. They listen to violet, smell red, and bring their findings to the paper. I play "Pachelbel's Canon" and they tell me about the woman in long white robes disappearing over a hill. I show them Miro's paintings and they create long rambling narratives of Italian

family reunions, the drowning of children during ocean voyages, bloody hunting accidents, and stolen flowers. I have become a California Poet in the Schools.

My own passion for the music of words is a gift I find deeply gratifying to pass along. If children encounter that music when they're young, perhaps, as it did for me, it will get into their blood, become part of their reality, and they will grow up believing it is "normal" to write poems. If we get to enough of them, we can change the world.

Gail Rudd Entrekin, Editor

DEDICATION

Child's Wheel

I was a whisper
  conceived in the golden time
  Summer
  turning
    to
      Fall
And mountains, the only ones
    silent enough
   heard me mumbling songs
  in my first unborn moment
But in this deep basin
  between Earth's rocky fingers
I could not stay long
    Fall
     to
       Winter
      to
        Spring

The next chapter begins
in a hospital bed
touched by the ocean breath
born in the emerald time
  Spring turning
  to Summer
Kelp castles and
driftwood fortresses
heard my songs bounce off cliffs
and ripple the ocean

And Summer
  to
    Fall
      to
        Spring
          to
            Summer again
7 times until I returned
  to the mountains.

    In a blink
        I had grown my own
            eyes
        my own
            voice
    and to rock peaks
        and cradles
I returned
        and returned
    Summer to
        Fall to
            Winter

Where an icy wind
    stole my songs
    made me afraid
        to raise my voice

And now the power
    of that speck of child
against jutting peaks
        returns with the hail

    rides the winds
      of midnight
   saturates me with
       the rain
   Child of salt water
      and rock
   words now lost
     in thunder

Jenny Gealey
9th grade, Mendocino Community School, Mendocino
Karin Faulkner, Poet/Teacher

Jenny wrote this poem two months before she was hit by a car and killed while walking along the road with her friends.

WILD WORLD

The Storm

I have purple and yellow boots.
Deer are in the forest.
Morning and evening fly by.
It becomes night.
Green and red forests lie upon the earth.
Jungles lie in the night with forests.
The moon shines like silver.
Mustangs run in the night air.
A storm is upon us.
The echo of thunder
scares me.
It starts snowing.
The orange shadow of my night light
keeps me safe.
My nightmares are like tunnels
to the moon!

Elena Garza
3rd grade, Petaluma Valley Day School, Petaluma
Terry Ehret, Poet/teacher

To Live

People must carry peace in their hearts,
clouds in their arms
and friendship in their dreams.

They must learn the ground will crumble
leaving them nowhere.

They must see that the rabbits stealing carrots
are careful of this world,

that people from behind bars are not.

They must hear the world going by them,

the world of the lizard scurrying away,
the lions ruling the jungle,
the gorilla hooting
and the cats playing.

They must know these things
to live.

Zoe Meharg
4th grade, San Francisco Day School, San Francisco
Gail Newman, Poet/teacher

Lightning

Black snow clouds
    bright yellow snake
hiding
 then slithering
      across the mad sky.

Spines
    on
       the
          white
             dragon's
                back.

Sky of gray pages
    torn
from the diary
    of the rain god.

Ms. Huey's kindergarten class
Yick Wo Elementary School, San Francisco
Maureen Kerl DiSavino, Poet/teacher

Warm Silence

    From the misty lake spring lavender hues
Emerging sky blue silvers
    Nearby drooping Forest Green desperado
The Louisiana rubies spring from the dying horizon

      Breaking the rich black silence is a burst of
Water reflecting orange reds.
    The heron clears the silk of the violet pond.

What color is silence?

Anna Cameron
7th & 8th grade, Inyo County CPITS Conference
Allison Hedge Coke, Poet/teacher

New Year Poem

(for Tan Chi-Wah)

hot sun for winter.
heavy blue sky pushes against
our shoulders.

ten thousand snow geese rest
in a field of broken rice stubble.

mountains & oceans roll through space.
the geese jump into the air
like a joyful shout,
HAH!
20 thousand wings fan past
the sun.

poets look up from their
little chores,
then words are written
and sent flying.

John Barbato
Poet/teacher
Nevada City

The Moon I See

The moon I see is a dry blueberry in a black bowl.
It's a hole in God's blanket, the eye of a black wolf.
It is a lost pearl from the sun's necklace,
God's eye opening and closing day by day.
The moon I see is a light in a dark attic,
a pendulum ticking back and forth.
It is a heart breaking
then loving again.

Claire Marana
4th grade, Parkmead Elementary School, Walnut Creek
Maureen Kerl DiSavino, Poet/teacher

Alive

She was down on her side and lowing,

lantern light flickered, straw blowing
slippery and wet, he was licked alive.
New legs held him wobbly and bowing.

Candace Van Vliet
9th grade, Ukiah High School, Ukiah
Ann Marie Samson, Poet/teacher

El Granzido Magico

Yo veo el pato en el pond
donde las ramas viven.
El pato es el calor de una manga de hule.
El es magico. El granza mucho
cuando arriva
en el cielo como un papalote.

The Magic Quack

I see the duck on the pond
where the frogs live.
The duck is yellow like a raincoat.
The duck is magic. He quacks a lot
when he flies
in the sky like a kite.

Diana Resendiz
3rd grade, San Pasqual Union School, Escondido
Brandon Cesmat, Poet/teacher

Sea Song

I am glad
for this day
drenched by sun
cooled by sea.

The late
afternoon breezes
come.
Seagull scavengers
stalk trashcans,
sand castles crumble.

Wet, purple-lipped children
sit by ocean's edge
laughing when white sea foam
tickles them.

We are beyond caring
what the clock reads
wishing time could stretch
like this long reaching of the sea as it comes to speak.
Roar and whisper are one.

Listen:
Even the wind   is carried away
on the crests — swallowed
by thunder tide.

Claudia Axel
Poet/teacher
Carlsbad

Walking with the Wolf

I'm walking with the wolf
He's tellling me to run with the river

The river is telling me to fly with the birds

The birds are telling me
to go see the great faces that I like

The great faces are tellilng me
to go find my rock

The rock tells me
you will live and rise

Meagan Banyard
5th grade, Dana Gray Elementary School, Fort Bragg
Karin Faulkner, Poet/teacher

The Rain

When the clouds make rain,
there is real thick thunder,
and it hurts the rain.
And the rain cries out its tears.
After the thick thunder stops going,
the rain still rains.
And then no one can go outside
because it makes big puddles
and goes up to your legs
because it's so big you can't even
go outside.
And you have to stay inside
with hot chocolate.
And the hot chocolate is so good.

Zaire Paterson
1st grade, Alamo Elementary School, San Francisco
Claudia Dudley, Poet/teacher

Untitled

Under
open
leaps
of daring
faith
feathers
birds

Andrea Henry
7th grade, Dr. Martin Luther King Academic Middle School, SF
Maureen Kerl DiSavino, Poet/teacher

Red Life

Inside
pale
mosquito's
mind:
must
find
red
life

Tyson Siddle
7th grade, Dr. Martin Luther King Academic Middle School, SF
Maureen Kerl DiSavino, Poet/teacher

At Night

Sleep closes your eyes.
Night, the dark thing.
The moon is like a light bulb.
Stars are sprinkles for the skies.
Dreams are the pictures on your brain.
Poetry, the sweet dreams
    you have in your mind.
Imagination, like ten kittens
    crossing down the lane
    that you
        live
            on.

Song-I Yang
2nd grade, Wade Thomas Elementary School, San Anselmo
Linda Strauss, Poet/teacher

Tender Mountains

I went up to the
tenderest mountains
there ever were.
I went fishing.
I actually caught one.
It was the tenderest
fish.
I looked up.
There was the bluest
sky and I said <u>if I ever</u>
go up there
it would be the
<u>tenderest sky</u>.
I said <u>maybe I can hear</u>
the stream go
<u>by and by.</u>

Jewinell Barlow
5th grade, Big Pine Elementary School, Big Pine
Judith Butler, Poet/teacher

STREETS

streets
black streets
black new streets
black new paved streets
black new paved good-smelling streets
black new paved good-smelling with a yellow dotted
line down the middle
streets

Amber Martin
5th grade, Ocean View Elementary School, Arroyo Grande
Toni Wynn, Poet/teacher

LEAF

When a leaf dies
it sounds like the wind moaning
for a leaf is more precious
than we expected.

Adina Fleming
      Santa Rosa
Maureen Hurley, Poet/teacher

Untitled

Dear ant,
I am
sorry
that
I ruined
your
home
but
it was
fun
I made
you mad
a lot
of ants
came
out and
it looked
like
hot
lava
coming
out of
a volcano.

Cullen Breuer-Harberts
3rd & 4th grade, Hooker Oak School, Chico
Amy Gaffney, Poet/teacher

The Rabbit

Nobody asked
me if I wanted
another serving of
carrots so I went
to bed hungry.
Nobody asked me
if I wanted hay on
me to keep me warm
so I was cold all
night. Nobody asked
me if I could swim
so I almost drowned.
Nobody asked me
if my feet were
sore so I went
Oh Ahh-ing all
the way home.

Nobody
asked me if
I was tired
so I fell
asleep with
my head in
my plate.
Nobody asked me
if I wanted
to wash
the food off my
face so it was
sticky. Nobody
asked me
if I felt

sick so I threw up in the crowd
of rabbits. Then everything changed
after that. They asked if I wanted
another serving of carrots. They asked
if I wanted hay to keep me warm.
They asked if I could swim so I
didn't drown. They asked me if my
feet were sore so I wouldn't yelp
in pain. They asked if I was tired
so I wouldn't get my face covered
in food. So if ever again they
don't ask me something all I have
to do is get sick.

Christina Girlando
3rd grade, Monte Vista School, Santa Barbara
Perie Longo, Poet/teacher

POWDER PINK

Powder Pink is from Hell.
Her mother's white, pure. Her father's
dragon blood. They met in death.
She does other people's hair for a living.
Powder Pink's favorite band is Slant 6.
Her favorite film is
"Belle de Jour."
Powder Pink flutters through the sky.
For vacation, she goes to D.C.
In five years, she wants
to be committed to Baby Blue.

Alexis Mourenza
10th grade, Pacific Beach Continuation High School, San Luis Obispo
Michael McLaughlin, Poet/teacher

CHRISTMAS IN A CALVIN KLEIN JUNGLE

A stain on my conscience that Spray n' Wash couldn't lift.
A heretic, I was, for I had broken the holiest of social vows.
Onward approached
        the heralded day that signifies
                the birth of Jesus-Christ ,
Yet I had forgotten to litter the socks of my loved ones with
tacky   knicknacks!
As I lay there, lethargic,
        a cloud licked my face, as if to say
                "A partridge in a pear treee! Quick!"
Trembling, I walked, I peered,
I searched like a fledgling child through racks of pines
        (all marked at 35% off retail!)
and sampled the polyester raspberries

(they were out of season).
Yuletide greeting glared at me with shaking-head malcontent.
Styrofoam snow simultaneously simulated the Nativity
        and yelled at me in arctic voices
            (no two the same!)
Sugar dripped from the mouth of a kindly asp.
He guided me toward the tree of the knowledge of all
designer-good   and generic-
evil.
It hulked over the perfume counter, smiling at me.
The wily serpent floated above the Chanel .
He squirted me with smelly fireworks
                that exploded in the sky!!! BOOM!!!
My flesh sizzled with quiet solemnity...

... it was at that point that I realized that I was naked ...

...And screeching eagles swooped down from behind the
cameras of   the Lord ,
peered from behind their sunglasses ...

    ... and kicked me out of Macy's .

Michael Baker
12th grade, Morse High School, San Diego
Glory Foster, Poet/teacher

INFINITY

What is the difference between
astronomically huge and microscopically small?
Just how much bigger does it get?
Does anyone really believe that we don't just die?
If the sun collapsed, do you really think
it would be such a sad thing?
What is infinity and why are we in it?
Do you think the big bang started everything, really?
Where are all these phenomena happening?
Are we just sitting on someone's kitchen floor,
a little atomic particle called the universe?
How much weirder does it get?
How much can we understand?
Does it ever end or never begin?
Time is insignificant. Space is insignificant.
This is what we are.
I wonder what time looks like from far away.

Diana Strong
10th grade, Mendocino Community School, Mendocino
Karin Faulkner, Poet/teacher

IN THE SKY

On the 5th floor, there
was a wonderful garden
with trees, roses, flowers,
plants, ponds, and grass.
On the 10th floor
there were unicorns,
fish and things that

are nice in fairy tales.
On the 15th floor
there was every kind
of animal. From a gerbil
to a giraffe. On the
20th floor I saw
dolphins that were happy
on land, seals, and
killer whales. On the
25th floor I saw giant
plants, a pumpkin the
size of a room, a
turnip the size of a
house. On the 30th
floor I saw rainbows.
The whole 30th floor was
a rainbow. On the 35th
floor I saw clouds
as fluffy as a marshmallow.
On the 40th floor I saw
the stars and moon. On the
45th floor I saw
a lagoon with swans,
willow trees, and the singing
of a bird. On the 50th
floor, the last floor,
were kittens. All kittens.
You couldn't even see
what they were sitting
on, there were so many.
A bird took me up there.
Two eagles. That's how I
got to the 50th floor.

Kari Hall
4th grade, Lafayette Elementary School, Lafayette
Alison Luterman, Poet/teacher

IN AFRICA

Sun,
red
in Africa.
The Cheetah
blinks
and rests its head.
Snake,
blinded by the Sun,
goes down its hole.
Me,
I walk,
my feet slowly press the grass.
I stop,
close my eyes,
and listen to the Thunder
far away
yet close
in my heart.
The rain starts
falling limply to the ground
splashing on my feet
small
white
feet.
The Sun sets
as the rain soaks
into the wet
soggy
brown
earth.

Brette Gentry
5th grade, Topanga Elementary School, Topanga
Sita Stulberg, Poet/teacher

CITY LIFE OF BOMBAY

Once again the cold morning breeze
in through the open doors.
Awake to the smell of
fresh baked flatbread
with mint chutney.
Out into the sticky heavy air.
Horns honking,
the low-toned call of the paper vendor,
fat crow on the balcony,
people running like madmen on the streets.
A beggar sits hopelessly in the middle of it all.
Shops lined up like ants.
An old woman on her balcony hangs out a cloth to dry.
And then, like a bucket of water
monsoon rain falls.
Everyone runs for cover,
and me, I sit smiling on my balcony
eating my warm flatbread.

Ajay Nayak
10th grade, Acalanes High School, Lafayette
Alison Luterman, Poet/teacher

Van Gogh's "Garden at St. Remy"

Do you remember the garden at St. Remy?
Do you remember how the wind
rustled in the branches of the trees
and blew through our clothes
bringing bright color to your cheeks?
Do you remember the cold stone bench
beneath the shivering trees
where we would sit, you and I,
and watch the sun sink beneath the hill,
staining the sky a fiery orange?
Do you remember how the trees
stretched so high up
that the leaves left smudges of green
on the blue of the sky?
But now the bench is empty.
The wind murmurs only to itself,
and the garden is blurred with tears.

Jill Fortuna
10th grade, International Studies High School, San Francisco
Susan Terence, Poet/teacher

Fields

Fields full of grass
  All slone,
  birds calling.
In Vietnam,
  kids dancing
    playing in the field
      full of rice
        tall stalks.
Birds flying everywhere
  hundreds of doves
    swooping down
    towards the kids.
I feel protected
  by the grandfather I never met,
    died at 32,
  leaving my mom,
    an innocent 5-year-old.
Leaving my grandma,
  going insane,
    my mom doing housework
  walking home alone from school
    at the age of 5.
  My grandma,
    beating my mom.
    My mom,
      running to the fields
      to get away.

E.D.
7th grade, Paul Revere Middle School, Venice
Sita Stulberg, Poet/teacher

The Rain Forest

People painting dark
canoes, turning into flying trees,
dancing deadly snakes
kill the green luscious plants,
poison dark, dark monkeys.
Art of birds gliding through the cactus grass,
green slimy grass, giant raining trees,
butterflies dark blue as water,
TREES ALL TREES NO LIGHT,
SWIM SWIM HOT ROOTS.
Big as the world chirp of call of the birds,
scary dark, dark to the begging of the blue old woman,
dark shadows of animals come come to the
rain forest wild.

Tim Lowe
5th grade, Vannoy Elementary School, Castro Valley
Janice De Ruiter, Poet/teacher

Gone

We're on a lake
It stinks real bad
maybe it's the fish
or the friends I'm with
The sun is blistering
We feel like we're going to melt
Fishing is like reading a book
I'm ticked that I have not caught a thing
so I throw my pole in
though Nick has caught at least twelve
Landon is playing his guitar
and doing something else and yelling
heaven knows why
I finally caught something
it was a 10-pound bass
Landon caught a root
he is so proud
I feel we're drifting out to sea

Zack Ziegler
7th grade, Bret Harte Middle School, San Jose
Kim Nelson, Poet/teacher

Lawn Chairs

Sadness lives in the basement
and the only way it can get up to
the kitchen where hatred lives is
to go through the stairway, and that's
where anger lives. And they mix it up, so
that all the feelings cover each other.
Loneliness is stuck in a closet. Frustration
is on the roof naked yelling and screaming.
Sometimes embarrassment puts a strait jacket on
him. Then he jumps off. And hyper is running
into all the rooms pissing people off.
Love sits in the living room waiting
for someone to sit down with him. Frightened comes
and takes up the seat. Happiness has
always been at the beach and plans
never to come back to the madness.
Lust was bad and only confusion
started talking to him. Both go over and
talk to love and team up with frightened
to make love move to the dog house!
Remorse only comes out when sadness and
anger do something stupid. And this house is
<u>really really small</u>.

Justin
Redwoods School, Probation Center, Watsonville
Kimberly Nelson, Poet/teacher

Woman

I see a woman.
Night is on her shoulders,
rags on her soul.
She seems not to notice
and hums a spellbinding song.
She jumps into the river.
The water takes her to the Arctic.
She goes under not to be seen again.
The sunlight spills down her.
Cold surrenders to the warmth.
She thinks about something
important, nothing at all.
All the hours of hard work
have healed and she goes into
that wonderful place we call dreams.

Addie Reyes
6th grade, Cabrillo Middle School, Ventura
Shelley Savren, Poet/teacher

Staying Warm

Early morning, she's still outside
and it's cold.
She'll smoke a cigarette and try to keep warm.
Discard that bottle, went flat
a long time ago.
How is it, on a night like last night,
beer gets warm but your fingers and toes freeze up solid?
She walks toward school. She can stay there
all day and be warm, maybe even scrounge up some food,
at least bum some money for cigarettes and beer.
It keeps her alive, at least she thinks it does.
She doesn't look around because her neck hurts
from no pillow and the cold.
I saw her out there three nights in a row,
pale face, sunken eyes. I offered her some coffee,
temptation creeping warmly from my house
and she couldn't refuse ...
Her nose ran as she thanked me and thanked me
and thanked me. I offered her a shower, no thanks,
she washed her hands and face and left me forever.
I wonder where she'll be this night and if she's warm.

Toni Bagley
11th grade, Ridgeway Continuation High School, Santa Rosa
Mike Tuggle, Poet/teacher

THE LADY IN PIECES

after a painting by Picasso

Crying, gasping, screaming,
her hat, her red hat,
like a speedboat,
like grey armor
around her face
and sad tears under her eyes.
She is biting her finger
because she is afraid.
Her hair looks like spider's legs.
She is alone,
and her eyes are open wide.
Her nose goes in, not out,
and she's all broken into pieces.
Her tears taste like salt
and her sadness is like
a bad dream.

Mrs. Allen's 1st grade class
McNear Elementary School, Petaluma
Terry Ehret, Poet/teacher

Cowboy Bill

I stroll through the corral,
trying to tolerate the smell
of fresh manure.
You ride up on your chocolate-dust horse.
I can almost taste the cigarette hanging
out the side of your chapped lips,
just by the smell.

I wonder if you like me.
I wonder if you notice how I stick out
like a sore thumb,
a city girl in your country world.

A cloud of smoke hangs about your
hat-topped head.
And the rolling green hills of Santa Paula
1919 spread spread out behind you,
as if they are streaming from
the back of your mind,
the setting of your memories.

I wonder how it could possibly be
that you are my grandfather,
a tough cowboy, a Marlboro man
with a red flannel and boots
and me a tender-footed stranger
who lives in a foreign world
and doesn't recognize you.

Evelyn Belasco
11th grade, Oxnard High School, Exnard
Shelley Savren, Poet/teacher

On My Way Home

Walking down Lake Street
the BMWs drive past,
confusing looks from their driver's eyes.
"What is she doing here?"
As a Lexus pulls up
the tinted windows go down,
classical music hits the air waves,
Chanel #5 hits my nose:
a woman with a matching poodle asks,
"Can I help you, dear?"
Responding, "No, I'm just going home."
Keep walking.
Young children with their nannies,
who I recognize from the Mission.
The nannies stop to say hi,
questioning why I'm here — worried.
I'm not here to cause trouble.
I just want to go home.

Jessy
Huckleberry House At-Risk-Youth Center, San Francisco
Teri Marquis, Poet/teacher

Angel Wings

Hair the color of bruised strawberries
sprinkled with sand stars
slender and freckled
16, 17 years
estimated by the size and shape of your bones.

What was in your pocket
so abruptly torn?
Could you have danced all night?
Who wouldn't know?
Who didn't care?

A crumpled ticket told
you rode Disneyland all day,
"The Happiest Place on Earth."

Your last $18 paid the taxi to the cliff.
Size 6 Nikes and a pink angora sweater
neatly folded at the edge,
nameless, you flew that moonless night.

What fine purple thread
divides your impetuous act
from my nights of terror?

Moving your arms repeatedly
in that bottom sand,
one last dance,
your angel wings reached for
anyone to care
anyone to name
your cold unclaimed body.

Yvonne Mason
Poet/teacher
Manhattan Beach

In Autumn

In autumn
I go outside and see
the maple leaves falling down
like cradles
rocking their way to the ground.

Nereida Gutierrez
4th grade, West Marin Elementary School, Novato
Terri Glass, Poet/teacher

My Influence

is like a beautiful disease
who leads me to conclusions
like a child in an amusement park
who becomes gray with smoke
is an eternal tie-dyed pipe
who is a time bomb
a dormant Zippo
who self-destructs every night
as he encourages me to.

Colleen Bruce
9th grade, International Studies Academy High School, San Francisco
Susan Terence, Poet/teacher

GIRL AT HUCK HOUSE, PAGE & LYON, SAN FRANCISCO

She carries around her attitude,
a heavy arsenal of
forget-you's, leave me alone's,
I don't need's ...
her skin so tight around her bones
that her mouth was squeezed in
after the fact
and sideways.
She explodes with black smoke
and, like some ancient serpent,
she coils and twists and leaps.
She has a flame thrower tongue.
Her universe spins too fast around,
speaking in tongues
she doesn't understand,
a foreign language.
Her only option is to kill on sight.
Good "de," girl: step on up
before they can come around behind ya.
Never let 'em see the weakness.

One hand shake won't do,
any missionary-style **how do you do,
I'll be your friend**.
Transparent.

This girl never sleeps.
Her dreams are awake
and her skin is awake and
her bones are awake and alive
and always screaming
and always ready to leap.

This girl has a mother with pink hair and tats —
Oh, no wonder.

Yeah, I bet you this girl is in prison by next year.
She's fourteen, plenty of time to run that train
all the way from **Juvi** to **CCWF**.
Throw away the key.

Something about this
thistle-tonged girl makes you want to
spit and slug and swallow hard
and bite on stones and play loud music
and say LEAVE ME ALONE.

Something about this girl
makes your eyes hot and
your skin and your heart.
If I got ahold of this girl
I'd probably squeeze her
so hard
she'd break.

Her mouth cracked wide open
like an egg.

Teri Marquis
Poet/teacher
San Francisco

With My Apologies

He clutches the pencil in his hand,
#2 Yellow Cascade,
pink eraser all rubbed down to a nub.
The pencil — he hates it,
doesn't feel right in his hand,
feels like barbed wire,
feels like water, uncontained,
feels like something squishy
 a mountain
 a bird
 a right answer.
Doesn't feel right, anyway.
Can't even get the point to hit the page.
He doesn't get it at all.
He gets distracted easily.
He wants to sharpen it.
He wants to go to the bathroom.
He wants to get a drink of water.
Can-I-get-a-drink-of-water?
Can-I-go-to-the-bathroom?
He doesn't want to wrap up
all of his words
in a piece of shiny white paper.
Too final.
Too perfect.
His words aren't right enough.
His words drown in his own voice.
His words are lies.
His words he can't tell his mother
or his girlfriend.
His words hit the lockers HARD
swirl around the combination —
 17R 6L 22R
don't forget the second spin.
His words spin

right off the page
can't stick
spin right off the edge of the world
if they could.
Nobody understands anyway.
His words can't fit into
 I love you
or **this is why** I did this.

His words hide under the desk,
the bed, in the closet,
under his tongue.
He'd just as soon never speak them
much less write them.
Just let them
stir up in his belly
like a hard driving rain.

Teri Marquis
Poet/teacher
San Francisco

9 A.M.

The children line up
single file
fingers poke
at classmates
they are learning

to draw
blood

with a No. 2 pencil
a back pocket bandana
with death row campaign ads
and support our troops
breakfast cereal.

At recess
they will untie Carl's shoe
twisting the lace
around the fat blue neck
of the lizard behind bungalow 15
they are learning

that this makes the teacher mad

like swastikas
and "North Side Little Hustlers"
scrawled on vocabulary skill sheets.

They will
drive by slowly

unrolling windows
flashing signs and bright blinding
mirrors

back at a nation
that kills for respect.

Mike Carlin
Poet/teacher
Temple City

Cuando Me Tumbaron

Cuando mis amigos me tumbaron
me senti tan lleno de lagrimas
como una casa con techo roto
en la lluvia.

When They Knocked Me Down

When my friends knocked me down
I felt as full of tears
as a house with a leaky roof
in the rain.

Juan Bautista
2nd grade, Thousand Oaks Elementary School, Berkeley

Poetry Teacher

lately, i am too full of lessons
fuses in one hand
matches in the other
discreet little sacks of
gunpowder under my tongue

explode a poem
a poem of fireworks
a noisy poem
a poem that burns your fingers
and makes your eyes water

i have poems crumpled
in the bottom of my purse
poems used as bookmarks in
anthologies of poems
poems on the back of bookmarks
poems on the front of bookmarks
lessons on bookmark poems:
short lines
few words
special typeface

so many lessons
how to write a poem on nothing
how to write a poem when it runs away from you
how to write a poem that tastes good
how to write a poem that smells funny
how to write a funny poem
how to make fun of a poe

i have so many lessons
cut words
add details
use texture

seek simplicity
be real
imagine the impossible
growl

turn into a poem
turn a poem into you

i am a teacher of poetry
a guide through contradictions
make your poem
now make it disappear

the poem lives
in that flash
between becoming
and dissolving

devorah major
Poet/teacher
San Francisco

ODE

You want them to write
an ode, a love song
to whatever delights
or defines them, and all they want
is to mock the drone
of the math teacher stuck in the fifties,
whose pants are too short and socks
are white. Or they want
to rattle off the slang
for their greatest curse,
their favorite sport,
the body parts that possess them
and which they yearn to possess,
the latest secret code of sex
they figure you can't decipher.
Or they want, simply,
to be left alone. Look
at this one, huddled inside
his arctic hood, asleep and slumped
toward the open window, explorer
of the other way. Or this one,
who recoils from being made
to speak the little she loves
for fear it will vanish, as so much
already has by her sixteenth year.
You too are afraid: that you don't have
what it takes to touch them
the way they need to be touched,
which is why you want them to do for themselves, praise
whatever sustains them, whatever
is good and doesn't go away.
And so, how can you not love them
when they answer with anti-odes:

to homework and take-homes,
to slow death by boredom, to the unspeakable
acts their bodies have endured for years
and for which they are only beginning
to find the pathetic and necessary words?
And on your last day, how can you
not love it when the quietest one
is changing at his locker
in a crowded hallway, teasing
the girls as he drops his pants,
the girls pretending they're in shock,
how can you hear him sing,
almost to himself, I'm the one

you love to hate — young boy smile
on a young man face, the old joy
of self-love still intact — how can you
hear him sing and not want to sing along,
not want to smile back?

Thomas Centolella
Poet/teacher
San Francisco

Teacher That Shines

for Mrs. Linda Hall

Teacher of mine, oh how you shine.
It's not a gleam or glisten,
a shimmer, sparkle, but a shine.
Not a diamond or jewel shine,
not any kind of earth shine.
It's a you shine,
and only you have your special shine.
people-feel-good shine.
A nice, warm, come-cuddle-me shine,
a loving, caring, funny, sharing shine.
It's a shine that you can keep to yourself,
or share-with-all-the-people shine.
It helps you feel good when you're not,
but for you, oh teacher of mine,
it's a mostly all the time shine.

Gabriel Catalfo
6th grade, Willard Middle School, Berkeley

WILD MIND

Joy

When it comes back to teach you
or you come back to learn
how half alive you've been,
how your own ignorance and arrogance
have kept you deprived —
when it comes back to you
or you yourself return,
joy is simple, unassuming.
Red tulips on their green stems.
Early spring vegetables, bright in the pan.
The primary colors of a child's painting,
the first lessons, all over again.

Thomas Centolella
Poet/Teacher
San Francisco

Flash of White Light

Once I saw a little tree that had a leaf at
the very top.
I looked at it and said nothing.
I thought about all the work and time that
went into the leaf and how in a split
second I could take it away.
I was powerful, but I didn't like it.
It was like a deranged puppet master
was controlling me and so
I wanted to break it but at the same time not
because I knew that I would regret it so
I stood there and tried to turn my left hand inside
out with a really tight fist.
It almost worked but I couldn't get it
just that little bit too tight so that
it suddenly disappeared then reappeared inside
out because that's what happens when something
is too much but only written bold and
the too that also means also, too.
When I try and remember certain things
I see a flash of white light and hear a pulsing
ringing-dinging sound that makes me think
of how I'm going to die.

Ross Hale
9th grade, Santa Barbara Music and Arts Conservatory, Santa Barbara
Perie Longo, Poet/Teacher

Red

Red sounds like a crackling fire on a cold winter's day.
It sounds like love and fear.
It sounds so inviting
yet it should have a danger sign on the door.
Red sounds soft yet loud.
Red sounds like sweet rock 'n roll music
echoing at all corners of the room.

Red smells like the girls that pass by you on the bus
that are wearing way too much perfume.
It smells like you're trying to tell someone something with
wearing   it
but you just don't know how to say it.
It can smell calm and soothing
but at the same time like you're yearning for excitement.

Red tastes like sweet blood from a fresh cut.
It tastes like that taste you just have to have but can't get.
It tastes wonderful in all ways if you love it.
If you hate it, even just the slightest bit,
it tastes like you're licking the asphalt when it's just been
poured.

Red looks exotic and rich with deep feelings.
It looks like it's trying to tell you something by staring into
your eyes
but it just can't get the words out.
It looks like your best friend
or your worst enemy.

Red feels like you're burning up
but ice cubes are covering your entire body.
It feels good, wonderful, yet a tad bit evil.
You like that way, even if you don't think so.
It feels right to wear it
but wrong to be a part of it.

Laura Albright-Wirtz
6th grade, Seven Hills School, Nevada City
Gail Rudd Entrekin, Poet/Teacher

The Wink

When you are winking at someone
you give them a flirting smile
that you like them.
To wink at someone means
you are trying
to make that person
fall into your hand
in an easy way,
and your eye
is closing
and opening
gently.

Chau Ta
7th-8th grade, West Point School, West Point
Lynn Crosbie Loux, Poet/Teacher

Flowers and Us

A flower.
It stands
alone.
It needs
its care like
you and me.
While people party,
people smile, people are
excited,
I sit here
writing about nature,
looking at land.
It makes me feel
sad.
People don't know
that land has feelings.
People don't
know it.
They are like flowers
who need
a lot of care.

Nixya Velasco
8th grade, Griffith Middle School, Los Angeles
Don Campbell, Poet/Teacher

Asleep in the House of Art

While I sleep in the house of art
words dream of me swimming,
dark fish below their surface

I am moving through the diastole of
dreams, sleeping in night's silvery pocket,
sleeping in the house of art

There are whole hours to squander
here waiting the ruturn of words
while swimming the dark below their surface

Tomorrow's words sink past last
night's lines long forgotten
while I sleep in the house of art

Words flying home, fluttering moths
at my heart's door, dark
words beating below the surface

Beating in and out of dreams
awaiting the return of those
still swimming below the dark, still dreaming

Sometimes some heart-pricking word breaks through,
draws blood from dreams
then rises above the surface
while I stay sleeping in the house of art.

Ann Marie Samson
Poet/teacher
Ukiah

A Vague Memory

A vague memory of a dim light and
long windy set of stairs gives a chill
running like a cheetah down my spine,
and a time long ago when black, black
as a deeply dark night and a sudden
blur of red gives me a dull pain
above my eye.

A time before I was even me,
I remember a blindness and had
to feel for my way around a
time before time was my time.

Matthew Ward
6th grade, Cohasset Elementary School, Chico
John Barbato, Poet/Teacher

In My Dream

In my dream I was a baby.
There was a bunch of birds that were big.
They took care of me.
They lived in an abandoned old stosre.
There were 25 or more.
They had powers of all sorts.
They taught them to me, all of the,
when I was about four years old.

Every night they would go aflight.
They would go through people's windows
to take food from people's houses.

There was a bird that was purple.
His hair went everywhere.
He was the guard.
Another bird was the most beautiful of them all.
He was "the leader of the pack."

I never really got to go out at night.
But then one warm night the leader asked
if I wanted to go with them.
So I said yes and I went.

As I glided through the night sky,
wings slapped against me,
but it felt good.
I could glide on and on and on.
Never before in my life had I felt so free.

Sara Heidelberger
4th grade, Deer Creek School, Nevada City
Gail Rudd Entrekin, Poet/Teacher

WHEAT

I stand behind a window
where lovers once built the only walls
still standing. A window.

There are no wheat fields
this close to the Pacific blue.

And though I toss live seed in the bricklined
geranium and canus beds each time
I winnow hulls from the bird feeder,
no tempest tousles its head toward
these grey steps, screened door.

Though there is seldom a time
I am without wheat.

Since childhood, it's been there — amber,
something straight
filling fields, reaping full futures,
flaxen. Since childhood,
shaking rustles,
seeds my mind with
gold and beige, with near colors,
void of closure, so

somewhere, in me, in the field fanning
outside this sashed and latex-painted window
wind patterns shaft and grain into full run.

Allison Hedge-Coke
Poet/Teacher
Santa Paula

Don't Forget to Breathe

I am a staring, scaring stretch of unbroken snow. Mountain river to the sky, spinning dreams, hopes of unforgotten storms, straight from the eye of a fighting, flirting, smelly skunk. I am a bully. Push, shove, a lone note, a music floating in amber pools of unidentified fluids. A low moan of sunshine, breaking the storm surface of swaying tree canopies, waiting; hate, hating the time of non-descriptive action carved in a sunstone of history. I like to lick peach-colored, lime-flavored faces, looking out into me through an invisible glass. My mind is melted into the brick red sky. My naval points west, my nose east. I sit standing backwards, inside out. I snicker and swivel, my hands combusting without any kind of plush warning. I long for someone to tell me I cannot, so that I have a blue excuse to show them I can. Dare me, I go. A yes is as good as a no. My feet patter on a flourescent noontime sidewalk, splattered in green and purple. The joker, of big balls, time, color, verbs, nouns, blurr together in a halo of untold questions, unstated statements. Everything is reversible: a stick has three multicolored ends, a square can have five corners if you see it from the right scarlet perspective. Snarl at me, I am begging you, please. A sapphire bicycle. I don't hit until you egg me on. But my revenge tastes ten times worse. Midnight blue flashes invade my mind. Last week I threw an automatic air conditioner out the window because it broke my train of thought. I have 50 thousand points of view. Crow black. Can you really tell your knees from your nose? I don't care anymore. Aqua fingertips. Everyone has their own style, she says, but the unofficial rule of life is: only loud ones make people listen. And I always get my way because I am the loudest of them all. I am a bossy, biting, booting, bully. I can walk on the ceiling, especially in the night. Chocolate brown. I am a mass confusion of navy blue and purple dreams. Can you breathe?

Terra Easton
7th-8th grade, West Point School, West Point
Lynn Crosbie Loux, Poet/teacher

Rattlesnake

My rattlesnake — he's only stuffed, but in my dream.
...ZZZ! He catches the burglar down
the street ... He happily slithers in the park ...
But never gets lost ... Snake swimming across
the pool, he snores on the bed when I'm not using
it during the day ... Wakes up at night.

Albert Linden
3rd grade, Tierra Santa Elementary School, San Diego
Joe Milosch, Poet/Teacher

Soy Jorge

Soy un diosito de amor.
Soy pajaros de lluvia
y velas de cascadas.
Soy un rey de la imaginacion
que quiere escribir.
Soy ojos.
Soy Jorge.

I Am Jorge

I am a little love god.
I am rain birds and
cascade candles.
I am a king of the imagination
who wants to write.
I am eyes.
I am Jorge.

Jorge Luis Hernandez
2nd grade, Thousand Oaks School, Berkeley
Margot Pepper, Poet/teacher

Soy Jennifer

Soy el oro de la selva
y pajaros de rosa;
estrellas de amor
y lluvia Azteca.
Soy besos de piano
como la lena roja.
Soy una palma de arena
brillando en el mar.
Soy flores de maiz azul majado
banandose en el rio.
Soy un sol de petalos.
Soy Jennifer.

I Am Jennifer

I'm the gold of the jungle
and rose birds;
stars of love
and Aztec rain.
I am piano kisses
like red firewood.
I am a sand palm
shining in the sea.
I am flowers of wet blue corn
bathing in the river.
I am a sun of petals.
I am Jennifer.

Jennifer Vasquez
2nd grade, Thousand Oaks School, Berkeley
Margot Pepper, Poet/teacher

Happiness

Happiness
makes me
jump on the
bed wearing
my pajamas
and makes
my cheeks
red.

Edwina Shin
2nd grade, Cabrillo Elementary School, San Francisco
Claudia Dudley, Poet/teacher

Annelisa's Poem

I'm a walking person
with angels inside me.
If they are walking angels,
they climb up my bones
and they get into my head.
They look through my eyes
and hear through my ears.

Annelisa Moe
Kindergarten, McNear Elementary School, Petaluma
Terry Ehret, Poet/teacher

I'm Standing Here, Now

on this rail of steel, looking down.
I see two rails, far apart.
On one stands my present situation, me,
the other, where I want to be.
Shall I leap from this rail to the other?

Looking back, I see the point where they converge
on the horizon, and I wonder
when did they separate?
Where did I let them separate?
Looking ahead, they converge again.
I can't turn back; I must reach that point ahead
where the rails meet once again.
I travel and travel.
But the rails remain parallel,
never deviating.
And the coveted point on the horizon remains there.
I hear the train at my back.

Ryan Steckler
12th grade, Ridgway Continuation High School, Santa Rosa
Mike Tuggle, Poet/teacher

Shy

Shy is when I go to
my mom and dad's
friends' house during
a holiday like New Year's Eve
and it is so noisy
I wish I could handcuff
the noise
and bring it
to jail.

Lauren Reda
2nd grade, Yick Wo Elementary School, San Francisco
Maureen Kerl DiSavino, Poet/teacher

Shyness

Shyness is an igloo with no door.
It is a pond so very quiet.
Shyness is a fire with no one wanting to touch it.
It is a circle never ending.
Shyness is a birthmark that will never go away.
It is an empty glass of milk.
Shyness is a pencil with no lead.
It is a heart with no heartbeat.
Shyness is the first day of school with
no apple to give the teacher.

Sharleen Esteves
6th grade, Valley Vista School, National City
Jon Sanford, Poet/teacher

STUTTER STUTTER

Why did you make me stutter
can't you see how far I got without it?
now I'm stuck with stutter problem
and repeating life over and over.
can't you see everyone hates me
because of you?
Why did you choose me for?
Now I'm a stutter kid who's repeating
over and over don't you know why.
I hate stuttering of the silent block
of bean you gave me don't you see
I'm going through a lot of therapy
of darkness of hateness
I dream that your soul and body
of your powerful voice
will combine in mine
of sadness of stuttering

Somkhit Thongban
8th grade, Hanna Boys Center School, Sonoma
Arthur Dawson, Poet/teacher

I Am Black

I am black in my dad's car
In your hair sleeping
In the stallion's mane running
In the chocolate bar melting
Whispering in your imagination
Screaming on your tire
Like magic.
I can run like the wind
Moving on a freeway
Hitting the ground with my hooves.
In the mountains I laugh
Crying when I am begging for food
I breathe the fresh air
I am black on the edge of the earth.

Sprigley Allan
2nd grade, Torrey Pines Elementary School, La Jolla
Steve Garber, Poet/teacher

My Heart

My heart is a tree
and it's trying
to get some wind.

Simon Christy
1st grade, Gault School, Santa Cruz
Patrice Vecchione, Poet/teacher

VIDA

I come from el corazon de Jesus.
I come from blood that was given to me.
I come from the love of my people,
my homeboys and girls.
I come from knowing if my choice
is to die or to go to jail.
I come from choices that make others
hurt & choices that bring others hate.
I come from a familia that can't
understand where I came from
because I come from two corazones.
I come from love that was never shown.
I come from hatred that was never said but known.
I come from the valley that gives me pride & respect.
I come from where my friends
have problems that I can't handle.
I come from trust.
I come from heaven and hell put together.
I come from where guys are cute
where girls cry for the guys
when love has been discovered but also broken
because death took over love.
I come from young to old.
I come from pain.
I come from being a proud Chicana.
I come from losing friends.
I come from where little boys
learn to use guns,
where the guns are guilty, and the boys innocent.
I come from a little girl becoming a young mother.
I come from el pueblito de Healdsburg.

Lorena Macias
6th grade, Alexander Valley School, Healdsburg
Maureen Hurley, Poet/teacher

What Can I Do?

An innocent child growing up in the winderness
living in a world of terror, hatred, and bitterness.
My mind was spinning. I couldn't comprehend.
Sometimes I wished that my life would journey to an end.
I was so sick, but I was tired of being sick.
My life was hanging from the edge of a cliff.
I was living in a world that people thought was crazy,
uneducated little girls out having babies,
little boys were on the corner ouside selling rock.
My mom used to ask me when will it ever stop,
but that was a question I just couldn't understand.
A youngster growing up in the ghetto already a grown man
surviving the game — that's what it's all about.
My mom went through pain keeping food in my family's
house.
But our great dream evaporated when Pops got a murder
case,
life with no parole. Never again would I see his face.
My life is living in terror and a lot of suspense.
But I can't do nothing, when I'm living behind a fence.

LaQuinta Clark
12th grade, Colston School, Ventura
Shelley Savren, Poet/teacher

Surreal Juxtapositions

I am the rainbow of pride
disappearing quietly into the cool
morning mist.

I am the strong, purple salmon
swimming happily up the flowing river
of peanut butter.

I am the crooked sidewalk of hope
    waiting on the blue moon
    to shine softly on my back.

I am the hopeless teacher
    running off the cliffs
    of frustration.

I am the furry frog flying crazily
through the soft clouds of wisdom.

I am the cool stream of wonder
flowing, floating through the sweet air.

I am the child of madness rolling
helplessly
    down the steep mountain of life.

Katie Hardin
7th grade, Grizzly Hill School, Nevada City
Will Staple, Poet/teacher

Mama Who

Mama who is a sleeping turtle walks on
Civic Center after a long day's work,
who likes to eat sole fish and sweet potatoes
while listening to the citizenship in her
Panasonic Walkman,
who asks me to translate her English lessons
from her night school,
who calls me Zhen and says, "Put more
clothes on, or else you'll get a cold,"
who is a heater that warms my heart —
who always puts a blanket on me when I fall asleep.
But sometimes a bitter, cold wind that hurts me deeply,
who thinks money is more important than me,
who blames for something I didn't do.
Mama who's my love, but also is a rock exploding in my
head.

Emily Chan
11th grade, International Studies Academy H.S., San Francisco
Susan Terence, Poet/teacher

GRANDMOTHER

I can see your shadow rolling
through the sky. I can hear you talking
to me, Grandma. I can believe you are
not dead in my word. I can stand
and hear the flow of wind swishing.
I can always keep enough memories
in my head. I can always see
your blue eyes staring at my face.
I can taste your heart going
through my veins. I can keep your key
for the door
for the life that you had.
I can love you like a tongue
loves candy.

Jeremiah Khaleq
4th grade, Yick Wo Elementary School, San Francisco
Maureen Kerl DiSavino, Poet/teacher

Potato Love

The pest exterminator kissed the potato
    because it was the only thing that wouldn't
slap his face
    for the dry smell of poison that filled the
air when he was near.

His eyes look like walnuts, and
    his shaggy beard hangs to his shoulders.
Maybe there is someone for him, but
    he's not expecting her
as he sits on the side of his bed,
    listening to the radio
in his dusty apartment.

Amy Williams
6th grade, San Pasqual Union School, San Pasqual Valley
Brandon Cesmat, Poet/teacher

FATHER

Ducking through the door,
striding across the room,
    he came.
His square face set with a smile,
    His eyes round and dark,
        sparkling by the light.
Five steps and he was across my living room.
    There I was standing,
        a smile on my face.
    There I was standing,
looking straight up for miles just to see his face.
His massive hand came down,
        lightly patting me on the head.
Using both hands,
    he effortlessly lifted me into the air.
    From way up there,
I saw my home in a whole new way.
I laughed, I giggled ... I was happy.
He said he couldn't stay long,
    but that was all right.
I knew he would be back,
    and that's all that mattered.
He placed me on the floor
    and said good-bye.
I watched him vanish that night,
    eight years to this day.

Cameron Brooks
11th grade, Oxnard High School, Oxnard
Shelley Savren, Poet/teacher

Finding Life

A red sun is drying the water.
The sun is so hot it's burning the floor.
People are going to die.
Last chance to give us work.
Do you want to die?
I pick no.
I want to go places.
I want to see winter.
I hear something open the door.
It's God.

Felipe Sanchez
4th grade, Hillside Elementary School, South San Francisco
Maureen Kerl DiSavino, Poet/teacher

Roben

Roben
is a tornado.
His personality
is a white pearl of unknown.
He is a soft wind, a daisy
floating downstream.
He says "what" and I can fly.
Underneath he is a bird.

Ian Maurer
5th grade, Dunbar Elementary School, Glen Ellen
Arthur Dawson, Poet/teacher

Marc of Courage

you were an old man at 14
your life was filled with abuse,
crimes committed by and against you
you were not in love
your gritty smile showed years of practice
anger seeped through your stylish clothes,
your bad boy role
we hardly knew each other,
both forced acquaintances in a place
we were forced to be, scraping to survive
you did not think of me
that day
as i did not think of you
you were not in love, but you found some
that day
at 5000 miles an hour
exploding steel love that dug a tunnel
through your eye

next i saw you satisfied,
pale faced and placed in your coffin
cousins and stepbrothers asked
how could we not have known?
a smile twinkled on your lipsticked mouth
death loved you now, unquestioningly

Jon Campbell
12th grade, Santa Rosa High School, Santa Rosa
Don Campbell, Poet/teacher

Pact

I.
The morning you came home
with them, I stood by the front door.
I was disappointed they made me
sit on the chair in the dining room,
all the way back on worn leather.
My legs dangling over the edge,
my hands folded neatly,
I waited there for you.
And when they finally handed you
down to me,
I moved your warm blanket back,
memorized the shape of your bald head,
counted the tiny lines and folds
of your new skin. I wanted to see
your eyes open to me,
hear your voice sing my name.
The weight of you
in my arms that first morning
was only the beginning —
the slow way our small lives
would turn from one another.

II.
Down the black road we kicked rocks,
fighting over who would lead
who would hold the rusted flashlight.
The wind racked over us,
the grass we walked through
eddied high and wet. I remember
how we kept stopping to make certain
it was only the cicadas hissing those songs
and when you were afraid

the dark was walking too close behind us,
I pretended I wasn't and kept watch
toward the lowering sky.
We made a thin trail to the water that night
and, as you put your hands into mine,
I pulled you in, not knowing
what I was doing, not knowing
it would take something stronger
to hold us together.

Karen Benke
Poet/teacher
Mill Valley

Alligator Tales

Early Saturday morning, still in our pajamas, my sister and I fly like lightening bugs into the living room. The curtains are open and sunlight blazes through the front window, making triangular patterns across the thick shag carpet. **The places the light touches are alligators. Don't step on the alligators**, I tell her. **They'll eat you!** I run around the couch to the over-stuffed armchair propped on wooden blocks. **Here it is. Here's the boat**, I announce, breathless. I climb aboard, stand on the torn cushion, look over the edge at all the alligators and — as my sister tries to scramble for safety — I set sail. **It's too late**, I holler, pushing her off. **Nooo**, she screams. **Wait for me**, she cries. **Alligators. Be careful of the alligators. They're going to eat you**, I wave. **Nooo**, she screams louder. **Girls**, our mother calls, her soft step moving toward us across the kitchen floor. Standing in the doorway, she shakes her head at me, bending to where my sister is locked in a wide, toothless scream. **She missed the boat**, I explain. **I can't help it if she missed the boat**. I pull my arms inside my nightgown and stare into the sea of green carpeting as sunlight floods the room. **The alligator bit me**, my sister wails, tears staining her rosy cheeks; she holds up her sleeve for our mother to inspect. **She wouldn't let me on the boat**, she points up at me, standing armless on the bow of our sinking.

Karen Benke
Poet/teacher,
Mill Valley

Late 20th Century: Spring

We went on the trolley:
my mother & I took the trolley from
where we lived out on greenfield street into
downtown los angeles where you could
then walk from one store to another &
to get your size right the shoe store
had a mahcine that you stepped up a
step to get to & you put your feet in an
opening in the bottom of the machine I
tell you this is true I remember the
red trolley & how when you look down
into or through the machine that was
inside the box your feet were in
you could see the bones of your feet they
were beautiful neon green which I guess is
the color x-rays are really I don't know
how those shoes fit or how I got home
or what my mother means when she says
california or what happened to the
trolley or the shoes or the machine but
everywhere in this green world my
feet take me now I see bones.

Jerry Martien
Poet/teacher
Arcata

When I First Saw the Girl

When I first saw the girl,
my eyes popped out from my face
and my heart started to play the drums
when she passed by.
I can smell her like a pack of roses.
When I am eating, I can see the girl
that I love most from a mile away
running in the green grass.
She is the only one that I love.

Otto Maldonado
4th grade, San Pedro School, San Rafael
Terri Glass, Poet/teacher

SKATING LIFE

Skating is a kind of
blood that flows through
me when I fly off
a ramp and skid
across the ground
in a fiery rage.

Andrew Wike
6th grade, Grand View School, Manhattan Beach
Yvonne Mason, Poet/teacher

Learning Spanish

I did not want to learn Spanish.
I hated the way
the words spilled out lazily
from my teacher's lips
like sleepy dogs,
even though English is unwieldy,
and sometimes,
consonants get jammed.

Spanish used to come like English,
only worse.
I choked on dieciocho and abuelito.
I swallowed double r's
and pronounced them
like I was from North Carolina.

But I have never had a language before
that tasted like horse
and felt like marshmallows.
I say things like:
La mesa con pollo, blanquios, calcuadora,
compra la radio y quiero ir afeitarse
a la casa anaranjado, for the Hell of it.
I still can't say anaranjado
without running out of breath.

I listen to my Mexican friends,
jealous and relieved.

When I speak Spanish,
I am much older —
maybe an old woman
about to die

spinning prayers like cotton,
and fading
into something like sand.

Sara Goodrich
10th grade, Aromas-San Juan High School, Gilroy
Patrice Vecchione, Poet/teacher

That Looks Good

I see my friend
eating an Oreo granola bar.
Suddenly my tummy starts to roar
saying oooo
that looks good!
I see him slowly
tearing a piece out
and putting it in his
mouth.
I'm so hungry
I can almost taste it.
So I go and ask him for
some.
My tummy
thanks me.
But then whispers
that was a small piece.

Abigail Abiog
10th grade, Marshall Fundamental School, Pasadena
Mike Carlin, Poet/teacher

SIMPLICITY

some things
    never fade and holding you close and pleasantly sweaty
on the   dance floor i wanted nothing more
than to
    squeeze myself inside of you embrace you with a need and
a force   big enough to crush us both and
not at
    all like the old days i wanted to kiss you with a kiss real
and fresh and undeniable, a question and an
answer and an unblemished future unfolding in one endless
dazzling   moment   i wanted to be
inside you
                       and i wanted to envelope you
        and i felt your heat like radiation thudding through
me   and i knew we shined beautiful once
more
                       and so i closed my eyes
             and i saw colors i couldn't explain
              and i saw leaves falling .
                   and i saw you
        and i had to steel myself to keep from shaking
and oh my god what we could have been why did you let me
go away?   why did you stop loving me the
instant treachery birthed itself in my eyes? i wanted to dance
with   you forever in denial of our blatant
impermanence slower and closer and tighter until we didn't
move at   all and just stood like pillars in each
other's arms, sure and real and indestructible

Jon Campbell
12th grade, Santa Rosa High School, Santa Rosa
Don Campbell, Poet/teacher

ARTICLES

The Pen is Mightier Than the Mouse

Karin Faulkner, Mendocino

Sometimes when I'm leaving a classroom after teaching a workshop, I hear the classroom teacher say, "Tomorrow we will be going into the computer lab and you can write some more poetry then." My gut gets tight and I have to bite my tongue to keep from saying, "Send them outside to the nearest trees to write. Later for the computer." Instinctively I simply want to protect kids from doing creative writing on the computer.

I fear the things that will happen if the new generation grows up trained to head for the computer to write, even though I am writing at the computer now. I want all of them to have years of practice indoors and out like I did with a pad of paper on their knees and a pen in their hands. I want them all to write sprawled out on the ground or in a tree. I want nothing in the way of the connection between self and self-expression.

Suppose we told children that the only way they could make a musical sound was to play the piano? What if we kept them from singing by saying, "No, not that way. Go over to the piano if you want to make music." They would learn to let the piano make the sound for them. Certainly there would be some kids who would become brilliant on the piano. But oh, so many more whose inner music died when it was not produced <u>by them</u>.

I think that the pencil is magic and when kids are coaxed to pick it up and GO someplace, the actual feel of the pencil in the fingers opens the heart and the scrape of it across the page reaches a deep spring where the true stuff flows. It is a personal act of freedom.

The urge for self-expression in kids is as innate as breathing. They all will sing their own songs, build with anything they can move, draw with anything on anything, paint with any wet material anywhere they find it and sculpt with anything malleable enough. Encouraged or merely allowed, this manipulating becomes a joyous, outpouring self-expression we call creativity, and later, Art.

Natural creativity gets altered when we channel it through the plastic boxes, wires and circuitry of the hot, new computer age. Some important processes get lost. Kids need to hold things in their hands, bend, and twist them, see how they change in front of the window light or held in the darkness between their two hands. They need to take it under the table with them or into the closet or bathtub. They need to run their tongue along things to see what that's like, see what happens if you add some spit to your paint. They need to rub what they are working with in their hair. They need to bite the crayon, smell the glue. It is part of their developmental process. They must try to get the cat interested in their finger painting. They have to read aloud to the dog. The computer may seem to be interactive, but we must not be tricked into believing the binary process gets involved with children's creativity.

What will be lost as more and more kids draw with colors in boxes on the screen that they click with their fingers on a gray plastic thing called (but having no relation to) a mouse? When we were little we chose the yellow crayon from the green and yellow box. We took it out with our fingers and applied it to the page. Today little Caitlin at the computer has her hand on the mouse. She sees the "page" on the screen. Step 1. She makes a flower by dragging the mouse which makes a line on the page. Step 2. She highlights the part of the flower she wants to make yellow. Step 3. She selects yellow from the boxes on the screen. Step 4. She clicks the mouse and the computer turns the flower yellow.

For Caitlin to pick up a crayon from the pile on the table would mean more than clicking on the yellow square with the mouse because she is actually doing it. The fingers holding the crayon make a depth of connection that is real. I am sure that the tactile sensations trigger things in the brain that stimulate several levels of learning. And cutting and pasting has to be done with scissors and glue by children, not by icons on a screen if they are going to learn what their hands and minds can do.

Forty-five years ago my parents got one of the very first televisions. Five years later my friends regualrly came over to our house to watch the family sit coms on Friday night. **Topper, I Remember Mama, The Milton Berle Show,** hot cocoa and popcorn. Five years later my father was involved in early planning for Educational Television. The dream was enormous. Nothing but good could happen to the television-watching children of the future. My father was proud to be part of the early meetings held at Georgetown University's Department of Education. Ten years later my father was dead. Twenty years later the average child has watched 18,000 murders on the tube by the time she is eighteen, and the average American preschool aged child is watching TV 4-5 hours a day. If my father knew what had become of television and its potential for educating children he would cry.

When I read, write, or draw, I feel that I am touching the infinite because I have gone far beyond myself **into realms I have made**. The combination of Me + My Creativity actually seems to take me outside time. I believe that is the magic formula which makes childhood's hours stretch so endlessly long. Time spent exploring one's own potential without a teacher, without a parent to helpfully interfere goes deeper than anything in a classroom. In contrast, I fear that Caitlin at the computer for hours will be learning only to manipulate it and to discover what she is capable of only in the computer's realm**.**

I'd wish for any kid more hours spent on the porch staring at clouds or beside a creek and digging his fingers in the dirt than at the keyboard and screen. Childhood's main task is to discover the world and one's place in it. Can a computer do that? The instantaneous answer I see to that question is a scene of young teen-age boys just inside the door at Safeway playing those ubiquitous video games. Last time I looked, one game was Ninja fighters, one punk street fighters, and the third a plane flying low and dropping bombs on targets.

"WOWBANG, BIG FUN, LONG DAY."

Jennifer Arin, San Francisco

Since this was my first time teaching poetry to ninth-graders, concerns pressed upon me. Would the poems I chose as examples be too complex, thus frustrating the easily-impatient teens? Or would they be too elementary, thus boring the impatient teens? Should I teach the well-crafted classics, or stick to the contemporary, or blend both? Above all, how could I introduce students to writing craft and technique without contaminating their originality, since I would be using prefabricated, "acceptable" poems as paradigms?

I decided to read the class some excerpts from Natalie Goldberg's books, **Wild Mind** and **Writing Down the Bones** because she promotes freedom in writing. Some of her advice: keep your hand moving across the page; don't hold back, go for what's scary; don't worry about spelling, grammar or punctuation; feel free to write the worst junk in America. I shared these ideas not as rules (anathema to any teen), but as pearls of wisdom. I also discussed the importance of imagination, line breaks, and detail.

I had heard, from reliable sources, that teens preoccupy themselves with fitting in, which means not standing out and, consequently, not participating in class (as this calls attention to the individual self). Like a performer going onstage for the first time, I feared facing a crowd of stoic or bored faces. I countered this eventuality by opening with a poem which validates individuality: "it's nice to be different/nice to be weird/being unique's not as bad as I feared." Then I told the students to write freestyle on that theme for five minutes.

To my delight, this warm-up served its purpose: loosening up students so they would feel all right about speaking up, speaking out. They responded enthusiastically, raised their hands frequently, and seemed surprisingly unself-conscious about sharing what they knew already about poetry. They were a bit reticent about asking questions, but I gave them permission to do so by making statements such as, "I don't know if I explained that clearly," and "Did I express it so it's understandable?" Thus they were freed from the notion that a lack of understanding translated into their lack of intelligence; they began to ask questions, and so to really learn.

In the following session, I again had them do a five-minute freestyle warm-up. The class loved this no-pressure writing, so we did it each time. I reviewed the aforementioned components of poetry (imagination, line breaks, detail), adding simile and metaphor to this list of "writers' techniques." I read a Shakespearean sonnet and a verse by David Ignatow to demonstrate simile, and to show how poetry can take many forms and has many disguises. I read one of my own humorous poems too, both so students would feel more free to share their own writing, and so they would respect me as a writer. Finally, I had them write their own humorous poems. I knew this exercise would be personal but still "safe" for them. (People often achieve distance through humor; psychologists call humor a "sophisticated defense.")

In the third class, I spoke of the virtue of showing, rather than telling. Note, for example, the following sentence: "The plane was about to take off, and he was afraid to fly." While we do receive interesting information, the words themselves are limp. A more riveting way to express the same idea is this: "As the grind of the plane's engines rose to a screech, he gasped for breath and grabbed the seatbelt with his sweaty palms." The sentence never states that the man is nervous, nor does it need to; we know this, and are drawn to the story and the character.

For variety, I took the students on a field trip the following week. They gathered five objects each. I read them some poems which relate objects to one another, rather than describe them as unconnected ("the whale teaches the crab how to sing," "the cave opens its sleepy eye to the bear.") Each student drew a flower with one of the gathered items on each petal, then did a poetic connect-the-dots from petal to petal, using words instead of drawn lines to connect the objects of the flower. This was to emphasize how the earth is a family of things, all cosmically related. I commented that it could be an emotional relationship, a social relationship, a spiritual connection or a physical one (physicists have discovered that all matter is made up of the same molecules, distinguishable only because of differing molecular structures).

I had guest poets visit the classroom so students would experience a range of styles and influences. I asked these guests to cover diverse elements of poetry, including repetition, alliteration, onomatopoeia, rhyme and half-rhyme, assonance and dissonance.

The penultimate class (incidentally, Spaniards say there is never a last time, only a next-to-last time), I brought with me a flamenco guitarist to accompany my Spanish dancing (I do this too, professionally). This was both to bring in a multi-ethnic aspect and to compare rhythm in poetry to musical rhythm. It provided a chance to speak of how poetry had, in "olden times," been sung or spoken to music, usually the strumming of a lyre. This created a bridge for discussion of poetic lyrics in today's music, from John Lennon's work to certain rap songs.

For the ultimate (final) lesson (I can say this since I'm not actually Spanish!), we threw a pizza and poetry party (in that order, too — we were all quite hungry after weeks of intellectual input and output!) After hands and desks were cleaned off, each student wrote one sentence about poetry. I then composed a group poem from their individual lines (their original wording is unchanged).

Upon my first visit to this class, I had asked students what they thought of poetry. Regrettably but predictably, they viewed poetry as "stupid" and "boring." I took the liberty of assuming the cause of this was that they didn't understand it. Too often, poetry is taught as a lofty and esoteric craft, a regal and almost archaic vehicle for writing which must be studied painstakingly in order to glean some meaning from it. My goal was to help poetry descend to earth. I would sooner have poetry seem like a mud puddle you can squish your toes in anytime, than a ray occasionally glimpsed on the horizon.

In contrast to their original opinions, here is what this group of students thought of poetry after only seven lessons:

Poetry is a walkway of words that fit
together like a hand in a glove.
My poems are like open books, open journeys.
My poems are wild with lots of imagination twisted inside.
My poems are wild and imaginative and reflect off my mind
in metallic colors of purple, green and pink.
Poetry is the pot of gold at the end of a rainbow.
Warm colors and soothing laughter float
into my life through poetry.
My poems can comfort you with the tender feeling of relief.
Poetry is my friend.
My poetry is wild and aggressive
like the tiger who hides behind
the tall grass waiting to attack its prey.
My poems are like birds soaring through
the spacious blue sky on a broiling hot summer day,
like the wind against my face on a hot summer's day.
My poems fly with the wind
and will make you fly oh so very high.
Poetry is flowing winds that whisper the secrets of magic.
My poems are like glowing yellow stars
in the deep, mysterious sky.
Poetry is a breath of cool, crisp, minty air
in a musty, stagnant world.
Poetry is active and alive.
Poetry is known worldwide.
When I write and reread my poems, I find
the eureka for living every time!
Poetry is a wowbang, big fun, long day.

-Class poem by Ms. Martinez's 9th grade class,
*Fall of '95, Sequoia High School,
Redwood City, California*

Earth Day: Worshipping Dirt

Terry Ehret, Petaluma

The poet Carolyn Kizer once said that great art is often provoked by great annoyance. That should be a tremendous comfort to us in this year of presidential campaigning, for although the visual, literary and performing artists can no longer hope for NEA grants to support our work, we can at least be assured of more than our share of annoyance from our politicians.

In fact, just recently the writer in me was moved by something deeper than annoyance at some of the campaign rhetoric of conservative Republican candidate Pat Buchanan. In a sound-bite portion of a New Hampshire speech, Mr. Buchanan voiced his concern for the moral decline of America's public schools, the result, undoubtedly, of the deplorable lack of Christian prayer in the classroom. Christmas, Mr. Buchanan explained, has been replaced by U.N. Day, when students might be asked to comtemplate, God forbid, world peace. And Easter, he continued, is equally ignored. Instead American schoolchildren now celebrate Earth Day ... (here Mr. Buchanan paused to allow the audience time to click their tongues collectively in disbelief, then finished) ... so we can all go out and worship **dirt**.

"Is this what the conservative Republican agenda has reduced the environmental movement to?" I wondered. For days, this speech and the audience laughter it provoked was repeated at each newscast on radio and T.V., and gradually what began as astonishment at this arrogant characterization of Earth Day mounted into irritation and disgust until I was seized with an urge to respond in some way to Mr. Buchanan. I'll write a letter to the editor, I thought. I'll write to Al Gore, whom George Bush dubbed "Ozone Man" in the last episode of presidential campaigning. He'll understand. I'll write the Sierra Club, the Nature Conservancy, Ducks Unlimited.

But, realizing the best way to disarm an enemy is to embrace him, I finally abandoned my letter-writing campaign and decided instead to write a poem -- a poem about worshipping dirt. It began with an idle thought while waiting in the palyground for parents to pick up their kindergartners. Several of them were flat on their stomachs, poking with fingers and twigs at t carck in the pavement, flicking up grainy crumbs of dirt lodged there. "We're freeing the dirt!" tget sgiyted ub a chorus. "Help us free the dirt!" I remembered then my own love affair with soil in the days before I learned about laundry. I formed my earthy-sacrament into pies, cakes, mud-iced and bruised-petal-decorated pastries, arranged on shelves in a neighbor's abandoned garden shed: my earliest altar. I went home and, in the cadences and endearments of Catholic prayer, I sang to dirt, that heaven toward which we are daily soughing.

The next week I brought the idea to my writing group, and we all wrote poems about dirt: fingernail dirt; Baudelairean metaphorical dirt; rich, aromatic compost-dirt; even the tired old political dirt candidates like Buchanan love to sling at each other. I brought it into my writing classes at the community college and the university, asking each s tudent to respond to the call to celebrate dirt. I went into the elementary school, to the kindergartners and fourth graders, exhorting them to empty their souls on the subject of dirt.

Yes, Pat Buchanan, our public schools are crawling with legions of dirt-worshippers! And for this outpouring of poetic creativity I am indebted to you. Out of the muck and mire of campaign rhetoric has sprung the flower of art. Thanks, Pat. These are for you.

THE DEEP, DEEP DOWN DIRT POEM
Before dirt was dirt, it was soil and appleseeds,
  turkey droppings and cow-poop.
Berfore dirt was dirt, it was leaves and rocks,
  sand and clouds.
If you throw it in the air, it comes down like dry rain.
On a hot day, dirt feels warm and soft under my feet.
My favorite dirt lives under my house,

in my basement, in the sandbox, in my backyard,
deep under the ocean.
In that dirt live worms and spiders,
  roly-poly bugs, roots of grass
  and sunflowers, and minty pine trees.
Dirt is so old, it might be a hundred,
  or a million, or two hundred.
If I listen deep, deep down, dirt's voice
  sounds squishy and thick like mud:
  "Blub, blub, blub."
The dust under the Titanic tells a story.
If I put my ear down close to the dirt,
its voice would be so loud,
everyone in the whole universe
could hear it.
Kindergarten students
McNear Elementary School, Petaluma

from **WE TALKED ABOUT DIRT AT THE FIRST SPRING MEETING OF THE COMMUNITY GARDEN BOARD OF DIRECTORS**
Our dirt here isn't real dirt

I think, as I dig a hole
to plant a new tree
and the sand slides back in
halfway to the top.
I grew up here,
on Union Street with a roof garden
and clay pots full of dirt
we carried up the stairs,
and then we moved to the red dirt
of our hill in Virginia
and the even redder, stickier
dirt around the raintree in Makalapa.
It never came out of the seat of my pants,
that red rust dirt.

And then in Chicago we planted the strip
beside the parking lot, and it was
black and rich, and
it grew the reddest geraniums I'd ever seen,
and now we're back to the
sand and sand hills
of the California coast, and dirt
becomes something to mix up,
like a recipe for bread: have
a little of this bone meal, have you tried
hoof and horn?

Susan Herron Sibbet

Art and Poetry

Glory Foster, San Diego

Before I begin this junior high or high school lesson, I play an aria by Maria Callas and talk about the importance of listening to different music than normally listened to. I relate the music to the movies "Babe" and "Shawshank Redemption," talking about the elevatiion of the human spirit.

Poets have always been inspired by works of Art. William Carlos Williams wrote "Pictures from Brueghel," Wallace Stevens "Man with a Blue Guitar" after Piccaso's work, and Ferlengetti "When I Look at Pictures." And, of course, here I discuss the most famous combiner of art and poetry, William Blake, and his belief in the uses of the five senses to discover the imagination.

I discuss the importance of opening oneself to a wide variety of art forms. If you listen to the same known music, read the same known literature, view the same known art, then all you do is recreate what is already known. I urge students to expose themselves to things beyond their understanding. The surrealist, Rene Magritte, says, "If you go to a museum to see what you always knew and understood then the mind does not advance. If an art work stops you and the mind has to grapple with meaning, that is the most important place to be. Then the mind grows and expands."

I point out how we've been trained out of grappling, and I show them works by Magritte, Gaugain, or Dali. I stress that there are no wrong or right answers. With art and poety, everything is possible. Gaugain said, "I shut my eyes in order to see." Van Gogh said, "My brush goes between my fingers as a bow on a violin." And Dali said, "Have no fear of perfection — you'll never reach it."

WRITING EXERCISE

1. Choose an art work from the circulating postcards or use

one of Magritte's.

2. Observe the painting very closely, noticing details, predominant colors, lines fuzzy or sharp, objects realistic or symbolic.

3. Write at least five lines about what you see or think you see or how you feel about what's going on in your imagination.

4. Explore the painting with your mind's eye. Try to sense its tone, mood, energy, place.

5. Think of anything you might know of the artist.

6. Imagine the artist in the act of creating the art work.

7. Allow all your senses to explore the art work.

This is the raw material for your poem. Write at least a 10-line poem on the painting.

Students have created exceptional poems from this exercise. I believe it is important to select surrealist artists because the discussion leads students into the realm of natural law and the violations of these laws they see in the paintings.

BIRD'S EYE VIEW
(after a painting by Dali)

The twisted mind of Dali,
twisting objects in mid-space.
A fruit bowl gone mad,
a swirling hurricane of thought
feeding off the white wine of longevity.

The homicidal knife,
stalking its cherry-shaped victim.
Shapes metamorphosing from the backdrop,
playing on your mind as children on a four-square court.
The solitary man,

trying to grasp the meaning
and only managing to hold a small piece.
Complete control amidst chaos.

Justin Markland, 10th grade,
Point Loma High School

PHENOMENON AT SEA

(after a painting by Ethel Greene)

Endless cycle of decomposition and reconstruction
Following strict criteria of reality
An endured reaction of the clash between amorphous
　elements
A continuous wheel of great momentum
All Elemental combinations are striving to change
　　the direction this tremendous momentum follows:
Yet never composed well enough to break this
　　cycles's endless pulse.
A runaway train of infinite mass and speed
Traveling through time and space
Never known in what parallel this train will come to its
　station:
　　Perhaps always

Stephen Olivas, 10th grade,
Point Loma High School

WRITING ABOUT FAMILY

Melissa Kwasny

Family. Can you think of anything more natural and, at the same time, more torturous to write about? Ask students to do this and invariably, the groans erupt, and well they should. Most of my public school students are experiencing difficulties in their families, from the pain of divorce or abandonment to squabbles with siblings, from sexual and physical violence to life in a series of foster homes. I used to walk around this subject as if it were a loaded gun until I realized that if I wanted my students to learn how to express their feelings, I couldn't find a topic that generates stronger ones.

For many students inexperienced with the forms of creative writing, the groans come as much from an inability to express feelings as from their pain at home. How to express something so complicated and intimate as relationship? Metaphor, I have found, is a powerful answer.

MY FAMILY

My brother is sad,
a closed door
with no knob to open it.
He hides on the other side
of the wall.
We rarely see him,
the real him, I mean,
the person with a heart.

Not that we don't watch
for him. See
how we circle around?
Even my grandmother,
brown cloud,
who thinks the worst of him.

My sister gets closest
of all. She is a cave
for him to rest in.
Once or twice
he has visited her
and spoken his secret truth.
My sister is a blue cave
or the legs of a blue animal
walking out of the picture.

My parents are alike in this,
red tears.
They bleed for him.
I crowd close,
hoping they will notice me.
I am a window
with two views of bright sky.

This poem is particularly effective because I introduce it as a poem about my brother who is "in trouble." Students of any age can relate so well to this that I have never had one ask me why. This poem somehow gives them freedom to talk about feelings that are not celebratory, especially if they have gotten the impression that poems are only about good feelings. "All feelings are good," I tell them.

For this lesson, an adaptation of a collage lesson by J. Ruth Gendler, you will need 8 1/2 x 11 inch tagboard, cut into quarters, one for each student, and piles of multi-colored construction paper, cut into eighths. You will also need glue or gluesticks and scissors. I ask students to: 1) Pick a color for each person in your family, 2) Cut a shape out of that color that represents what that person is like or is like to you, 3) Arrange the shapes on the tag board in a way that represents how your family is together. For example, are they all crowded together or each in his/her own corner? Are some closer than others? Is one person alone? Then, glue the shapes on the board and write a poem either on the back or around the shapes. For each person, describe the metaphor you have chosen and explain why you chose it. (My sister is a moon because she only shows me one side of her at a time.)

It helps enormously if you have made a collage of your own or for one of the sample poems. And make sure you give your students a time by which they should finish the artwork and start working on the poem. If I am teaching stanzas, I have them write about one person in each stanza.

MY FAMILY

I am a shoe
I step on my sister
She is the ground

My parents are
the puzzle pieces
because they are
divorced and they
don't go together

And the hearts
they try to
stay under us
to keep us up

by Jeffrey Cheng, 4th grade
Commodore/Sloat School

Another effective way to teach metaphor and talk about family at the same time is through the introduction of the concept of a family tree. For many of my ESL students, this is the first time they have encountered this term. What is it about a family that is like a tree? What is it about a tree that is like a family? Draw a diagram on the board and label roots, branches, trunk, leaves, etc. Who are the ancestors and why? Who is the trunk, the leaves, the apples? The spots on the apples? What if, instead of a family tree, we had a family sky? The students help me make a list on the board of things in the sky: rain, rainbow, storm cloud, sun. I ask them what represents them and why. What about their mother or father? I read them Ruth Forman's "Waiting on Summer:"

> Daddy is
> thunder with the brothers
> light rain with the sisters
> n lightning with me n Richie
> if we dance on the living room floor

What if we had a family ocean, family jungle, a family orchestra or garden or arboretum? I ask them to write a poem, using any of the metaphors on the board, mixing categories, sticking with them, or making up their own, and again, telling the reader why that metaphor fits.

Most importantly, I tell my students this: Family, at least for today, is whoever you choose it to be. Most of us don't live with our mother, father, sister, brother. Some grow up with a grandmother, like I did, or have aunties as close to them as a sister. Some live with their fathers. Some have never seen their fathers. Some live in foster homes. If there is someone you don't want to include, you don't have to. If there is someone who feels like family and is not a blood relative, that's fine, too. Family is, for better or worse, who we depend on.

BIBLIOGRAPHY

BIBLIOGRAPHY

The following list is meant as a teaching tool rather than an exhaustive compendium. Use it along with your own ideas, reading, writing, and intuition.

BOOK SOURCES

California Poets in the Schools
870 Market Street, Suite 1148
San Francisco, CA 94102
(415) 399-1565

California Poets in the Schools features yearly anthologies of student and poet-teacher poetry from 1981 to the present. The last three publications are *Remembering What Happened*, ©1991, *Snow We Might See in the Desert*, ©1992 and *On The Other Side of the Window*, ©1993. Each of these anthologies also contains lessons and essays on the art of teaching poetry writing. (Availability of some anthologies may be limited.) Expanded Poetry Education Catalogue available. Also a separate lesson plan series will be released in the fall of 1994.

OYATE
2702 Mathews Street
Berkeley, CA 94702
(510) 848-6700

An organization of Elders, artists, activists, educators and writers who have come together to bring the real histories of the indigenous peoples of this continent to the attention of all Americans. Texts, resources books, fiction, poetry, children's books and materials written and illustrated by Native people. Write for a catalogue, which includes storytelling work by Joseph Bruchac and poetry by Mary TallMountain. There's even a 1990 book called Basic Skills Caucasian Americans Workbook by Beverly Slapin.

Small Press Traffic
3599-24th Street
San Francisco, CA 94110

Small Press Traffic is an excellent source of literary magazines and small press publications of poetry, most of which you can't find in larger bookstores.

Teachers and Writers Collaborative
5 Union Square West
New York, NY 10003-3306

Teachers and Writers has an excellent catalogue of books about teaching writing, many of them which Teachers and Writers publishes. They also publish a magazine with articles, lessons and essays about teaching writing. A highly recommended source.

VIDEO SOURCE

The American Poetry Archives
The Poetry Center
San Francisco State University
1600 Holloway Avenue
San Francisco, CA 94132
(415) 338-1056

The American Poetry Archives rents and sells videotapes of all the poetry readings made by the Poetry Center since 1973, as well as of readings and interviews from the *Lannan Literary Series*, and of the outtakes of the 1960s NET series *USA: Poetry*, which consists of extensive interviews with major poets of that time, such as Charles Olson and Anne Sexton. An excellent way for students to see a wide range of varying backgrounds, styles, and voices. Catalogue available.

RECOMMENDED TEXTS

The Discovery of Poetry, Frances Mayes, ©1987, Harcourt Brace Jovanovich. A new text on the reading and writing of poetry, with a clear and tasteful introduction to the art and craft of poetry, "the language art," as the author tells us in her introduction.

For the Good of the Earth and Sun, Georgia Heard, ©1989, Heinemann. A very good text for teaching poetry to grades K–12. Many exercises and process notes. Offers a method for teaching poetry that respects the intelligence and originality of both teacher and student.

The Poetry Connection: An Anthology of Contemporary Poems with Ideas to Stimulate Children's Writing, Kinereth Gensler & Nina Nyhart. An excellent double anthology of adult and children's poetry cross-indexed with lessons and teaching approaches.

Poetry Inside and Out, Gail Newman and Judy Bebelaar, ©1987. Fifteen easy-to-follow poetry lessons complete with sample student poems.

Starting With Little Things, A Guide to Writing Poetry in the Classroom, Ingrid Wendt. Oregon Arts Foundation, 2111 Front Street, N.E., Suite 210, Salem, OR 97303. A well-organized and practical handbook with fifteen lessons, commentary, and poems by Oregon writers.

Writing Poetry, Barbara Drake, ©1983, Harcourt Brace Jovanovich. A solid handbook with twelve chapters full of teaching ideas, suggestions for writing, sample poems, a section on publishing, and a short bibliography.

The Art of Writing : A Guide for Poets, Students. and Readers by William Packard, St. Martin's Press, N.Y. ©1992. Karl Shapiro writes that this book is a classic among how-to books of writing poetry. It includes not only the history of poetry, and poetic devices but writing challenges to develop form and style, and remarks by dozens of poets.

Bay Leaf and Fool's Gold
Califia's Children
Dancing on the Brink of the World
It Begins With Me
Before and After My Cry, edited by Carolyn Lau

John Oliver Simon
California Heritage Program
2209 California Street
Berkeley, CA 94703

These books, put together during a model project in Oakland, California, used the resources of the Oakland Museum's three galleries of art, history and natural science to create an integrated poetry curriculum. Many lessons, student poems, and a bibliography.

CLASSIC TEXTS ABOUT TEACHING POETRY AND POETRY-WRITING TO CHILDREN

Children Write Poetry: A Creative Approach, 1951, 1967, Flora J. Arnstein, Dover Books.
Creative Power, Hughes Mearnes, 1929, Dover Books.
Getting from Here to There: Writing and Reading Poetry, Florence Grossman, Boynton/Cook Publishers.
Sound and Sense, An Introduction to Poetry, 1956, Laurence Perrine, Harcourt Brace Jovanovich.
Wishes, Lies, and Dreams, 1970, and *Rose, Where Did You Get That Red?*, 1973, Kenneth Koch, Vintage Books, Random House.

RECOMMENDED READING

Against Forgetting, 20th Century Poetry of Witness, © 1993, Carolyn Forché, Editor, W.W. Norton & Co., publisher. This powerful anthology includes 140 poets from 5 continents covering the topic of how the human spirit prevails in the midst of war and political injustice during this last century.

Anthology of 20th Century Native American Poetry, ©1988, Duane Niatum, Editor, Harper San Francisco. This book presents poetry of historic witness by the best of 36 Native American poets from James Welch to Joy Harjo.

AYUMI, A Japanese American Anthology, ©1980, P.O. Box 5024, San Francisco, CA 94101. Beautifully designed anthology of graphic and written work by four generations of Japanese Americans. Includes biographical information.

Black Sister, Erlene Stenton, Editor, Indiana University Press, Indiana. This is the only existing collection which includes the first poem written by an African-American woman in the 1700's, moving through African-American women's writing in the 1980's. A feast of poetry by African-American women.

Black Women Writers, ©1984, Mari Evans, Editor, Anchor Books, New York. A collection with insight and biographical and bibliographical information useful in introducing these writers to students.

Ca Dao Vietnam, A Bilingual Anthology. A bilingual anthology of Ca Dao, an ancient short lyric form heretofore passed on only orally. Offers a refreshing complement to haiku and other short forms.

Califia, the California Poetry, ©1979, Ishmael Reed, Editor. Available from Small Press Traffic. A lively, one-of-a-kind poetry collection from over 200 California writers from the 1800's to the 1970's. Particularly useful as a multicultural resource.

California Childhood: Recollections and Stories of the Golden State, ©1988, Gary Soto, Editor, Creative Arts Book Company, 833 Bancroft Way, Berkeley, CA 94710. A lively collection of essays, stories, and recollections with such writers as Genny Lim, devorah major, and Floyd Salas. The text can be combined with poetry writing lessons that look at childhood memories, geographical roots and cultural definition.

The Graywolf Annual Five: Multicultural Literacy, Opening the American Mind, Rick Simonson and Scott Walker, Editors, Graywolf Press, P.O. Box 75006, St. Paul, MN 55175. An extremely strong collection of essays which expands America's narrow view of her culture. Includes outstanding writers from the range of America's cultures writing on cultural issues. Especially suitable for teachers and high-school students.

Island: Poetry and History of Chinese Immigrants on Angel Island, 1910-1940, Hoc Doy Publishers. Order from your bookstore or through the San Francisco Study Center, 1095 Market Street, Suite 620, San Francisco, CA 94102. Poetry and longings of Chinese interred on Angel Island, the Ellis Island of the West, during a thirty-year period. Important as history and literature.

Knock at a Star: A Child's Introduction to Poetry, X.J. Kennedy and Dorothy M. Kennedy, Editors, ©1982, Little Brown and Co. A magnificently illustrated strong collection of poetry by well-known poets from William Blake and Walt Whitman to Gwendolyn Brooks and Langston Hughes.

Life Doesn't Frighten Me At All, poems compiled by John Agard, Henry Holt and Company, N.Y. ©1989. A wonderful anthology of multi-cultural poetry for young people.

News of the Universe, Poems of Twofold Consciousness, ©1980, chosen and edited by Robert Bly, Sierra Club Books, San Francisco.

Puerto Rican Writers at home in the USA, ©1991, Faythe Turner, Editor, Open Hand Publishing Inc., Seattle, WA. Richly textured poetry and prose of authentic Puerto Rican expression in contemporary America.

Talking to the Sun, Kenneth Koch and Kate Farrell, Editors, Metropolitan Museum of Art/Henry Holt & Co., N.Y. ©1985. Includes paintings, poems and writing suggestions.

The Open Boat, Garret Hongo, editor, Anchor Doubleday. Includes Asian American, Filipino and Indian poets.

The Place My Words Are Looking For, Poetry selected by Paul B. Janeczcho, Bradbury Press, N.Y. ©1990. Thirty nine of our leading poets present their poems as well as provide their thoughts, inspirations, anecdotes and memories about what it means to be a poet.

Without Names, ©1985, Kearney Street Workshop Press/Bay Area Filipino Writers, 827 Kearney Street, Box 3, San Francisco, CA 94133. A collection of Fifteen Bay Area Filipino American poets whose direct and imaginistic poetry can be geared to junior and high-school students.

PERIODICALS FOR STUDENTS
Compiled by **Maureen Kerl DiSavino**

Dear Student-Poets,

Here are some magazines that accept children's finished poems—poems that you have rewritten, typed out, and properly spelled and checked over. Send your best work. When you send your poems to a magazine, remember:

1. Include a coversheet with your name and home address and phone number; your grade, school, school address and phone number; and teacher name if appropriate;
2. Send a self-addressed, stamped enveloped (SASE) (big enough and with enough postage) so that the editors can return your work if they don't choose to use it. Don't be discouraged! Many writers get rejection slips, even your own poet-teachers;
3. Type your full name, address, school and age on each poem. If your poem is more than one page, put this information on each page;
4. Be patient. Good luck! Keep trying! Keep writing!

Children's Digest, Box 567, Indianapolis, IN 46206
Publishes eight times a year. Requires a letter from your parent or teacher stating that the work is original. Payment in copies and special subscription rate, prints about 30 poems per year. Send SASE. Reports in eight to ten weeks. Editor's advice: Keep trying!

Creative Kids, Box 6448, Mobile AL 36660
Publishes eight times a year, ages 5-18. Each piece must be labeled with the student's name, birth date, address and school address. Reports back in four weeks, pays in free magazine. A recent school picture is a good idea. Sometimes an accepted work will take a long time to get into print, depending on the theme of your poem. Editor's advice: Keep trying!

Highlights for Children, 803 Church Street, Honesdale, PA 18431.
Publishes eleven times a year, prints ten to fifteen poems per issue. Also publishes adult articles. Tries to respond in four weeks. Grades K-12. Along with your name and address, put your age.

Merlyn's Pen, P.O. Box 1058, East Greenwich, CT 02818
Publishes four times a year. Accepts all forms of writing and artwork from students grades 7-12. Coversheet and SASE required. Responds to all submissions, usually within ten weeks. Payment: 3 copies of magazine.

Stone Soup, The Magazine for Children, Children's Art Foundation, Box 83, Santa Cruz, CA 95063. Publishes five times a year. Accepts poems, stories, artwork, and book reviews by children. Age limit: 13. Reporting time: four weeks. Payment in copies and cash. Editor's advice: Read a few issues to find out if your work is suitable for the magazine. Send a SASE.

Voices of Youth, P.O. Box JJ, Sonoma, CA 95476
Publishes four times a year. Accepts all forms of writing and artwork from students grades 9-12. Must be typed. Acknowledges receipt of submissions; holds work until end of year if not published, then returns (SASE required). Payment: 1 copy of magazine.

CALIFORNIA POETS IN THE SCHOOLS

BOARD OF DIRECTORS

Tobey Kaplan	*President, Poet-Teacher* and *Area Coordinator*, Alameda County
David Simons	*Vice President, Attorney*, Cooper, White & Cooper, San Francisco
Carla Cogan	*Marketing*, Cooper, White and Cooper, San Francisco
Maureen Hurley	*Poet-Teacher*, Forestville
June Jordan	*Poet; Playwright; Political Activist; Professor of African-American Studies*, University of California, Berkeley
Susan Sibbet	*Poet-Teacher*, San Francisco
Toni Wynn	*Poet-Teacher*, San Luis Obispo

STAFF

Pamela Satterwhite	*Executive Director*
Greg McCombs	*Development and Member Services*

THERE'S NO BETTER INVESTMENT.

CPITS needs your support. There are many ways you can help:

CALIFORNIA
POETS IN THE
SCHOOLS

- Support your local poets!
- Encourage the creative writing, critical thinking and self esteem of our children.
- Take time for your own poetry.
- Share and affirm the diversity of California by insuring that our schools bring culturally competent poets and multicultural materials into the classroom.
- Build partnerships between schools, the community, and poets and artists.

...*And of course*, become a *Friend of CPITS*. Please join at whatever level you can afford:

- ☐ $10,000 Angel
- ☐ $5000 Laureate
- ☐ $1000 Benefactor
- ☐ $500 Patron
- ☐ $250 Leader
- ☐ $100 Sponsor
- ☐ $50 Associate/Org.
- ☐ $35 Contributor

Name _____

Address _____

City/State/Zip _____

Phone (day) ____-_____ (eve) ____-_____

Signature _____ Date _____

VISA/MC # ☐☐☐☐ ☐☐☐☐ ☐☐☐☐ ☐☐☐☐ Expires on ____

Contributions of $35 or more will receive the current edition of CPITS' Statewide Anthology—the best of the amazing poetry children produce in CPITS' workshops annually all over the state. Make checks payable to CPITS, 870 Market Street, Suite 1148, San Francisco, CA 94102.

- ☐ Please send me more information on CPITS.
- ☐ I am a teacher. I teach at _____
  in the county of _____
  school address _____ phone ____-____
- ☐ I'd like to sponsor a poet residency for our school.
- ☐ I'd like to volunteer. Please contact me.
- ☐ My employer (or spouse's employer) will match my contribution to California Poets in the Schools.
- ☐ Enclosed is my signed matching gift form.

Your contribution to CPITS is Tax-Deductible.

PLEASE MAKE CHECKS PAYABLE TO: CALIFORNIA POETS IN THE SCHOOLS
For more information, please call us at 415.399.1565 **THANK YOU!**